From

The Women's Press Ltd
34 Great Sutton Street, London EC1V 0DX

D0774496

Janet Ford is a Senior Lecturer in Sociology at Loughborough University, where she has worked since 1968. Her main areas of concern are the city and housing, particularly building societies and the allocation of owner occupation, and the workings of the labour market.

Ruth Sinclair is a Research Officer for Leicestershire County Council. She is actively involved in the Child Poverty Action Group and in Homestart. Her research interests have included decision-making for children in care and evaluating the role of community mental health teams in improving the provision of services to mentally handicapped people.

JANET FORD
AND RUTH SINCLAIR

Sixty Years On

Women Talk About Old Age

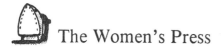 The Women's Press

First published by The Women's Press Limited 1987
A member of the Namara Group
34 Great Sutton Street, London EC1V 0DX

British Library Cataloguing in Publication Data

Ford, Janet
  Sixty years on: women talk about old age.
  1. Old age
  I. Title   II. Sinclair, Ruth
  305.2'6'0922   HQ1061

  ISBN 0-7043-4052-6

Typeset by Boldface Typesetters, London EC1
Printed and bound in Great Britain by
Hazell Watson & Viney Ltd., Aylesbury,
Bucks.

Contents

1
Ageism and Older Women

Stereotypes and older women

Most women in Britain can hope to live well beyond 60, the age at which we are officially labelled old, eligible for a pension, and expected to retire from paid employment. From 60 onwards we shall in all probability be referred to as 'elderly', 'retired' and 'O A P s' by the rest of society. In the west these terms form part of the stereotype about older people, who are seen as unproductive, dependent, restricted in their lives, and therefore not very interesting. How often in this country are older people seen as a fund of knowledge and wisdom, people to turn to for advice? How often are they the focus of our interest and curiosity? Not very often, it would seem. In some societies age gives status, so that only those towards the end of their lives are regarded as having enough experience and wisdom to deal with the most important issues and crises in their societies. We, however, have successfully deprived age of authority and of interest.

The western stereotypes of ageing and the old are prejudicial and discriminatory. Referring specifically to women a recent newspaper article commented: 'Here in Britain, as elsewhere, older women are regarded at best as amiable old ladies, at worst as a group of weak and defenceless pensioners. The label is unjust, unkind and unsuitable.'[1] The danger of such stereotyping, as with all labels, is that the elderly, perceiving that society has little regard for them, thus come to have little regard for themselves. As one of the people interviewed for this book said very clearly: 'What makes it harder is that other people think that old age is a write-off.'

In large part this situation exists because the dominant values within society stress productivity, a contribution to the wealth of society through work, achievement and competition. Even when people are no longer allowed to work (as with compulsory retirement), choose not to work, or are unable to work, they continue to be judged in terms of these values. Western societies have very ambivalent attitudes to leisure, even when it is regarded as 'having been earned'. We do not seem to have any idea how to talk or think about leisure or non-work in ways that give it status and see it as legitimate in its own right. Rather we tend to talk pejoratively of people with 'time on their hands', or to place the discussion of leisure within the framework provided by the dominant norms and search for ways to make leisure 'constructive and productive'. Referring specifically to the elderly, one writer says: 'A life of leisure is not a socially recognised virtue in our contemporary society . . . retired people are too often left alone to live out a presumed dotage.'[2]

Both men and women suffer from these stereotypes, but they are particularly detrimental to women because they add to their already disadvantaged position in terms of status, power and rewards. Women are often discounted in any consideration of the elderly. In extreme cases they are ignored, literally. A more common attitude is that their experiences can be understood without recourse to investigation, either because it is assumed that the pattern of their earlier life is continued into old age or that the findings from studies of men in old age can be extended to cover women. This has been the case with many studies of retirement, so that as late as 1982 Szcinovacs, editing a book of studies on women's retirement, commented that this was the first collection in the area, and that

women's retirement has been neglected because a major stumbling block was the belief that it did not constitute a

2

salient social or research issue, backed up by the highly questionable but prevalent assumption that retirement from work is a less significant event in women's lives.[3]

The disadvantaged position of women in terms of status, power and rewards is compounded for black women. Associated with low status and lack of interest, we find exaggerated, inappropriate stereotypes that flourish unchallenged through a lack of intimate knowledge. The voice of older black women is rarely given a chance to be heard.

Also hidden within the stereotype is insufficient recognition that old age can encompass a span of more than 30 years, and that the old are not one homogenous group. They exhibit great variety in the way they live and during this lengthy period of retirement can experience marked changes. For most of us 61 almost certainly differs in its implications from 80 or 90. For those who have worked, retirement can be a very lengthy period, for some as long as they spent in paid employment. For women this is increasingly the case as they come to form an ever larger percentage of the population over 80. Whilst recognising the variety among the elderly, we cannot escape the likelihood that there will be an inevitable closing in of physical capabilities and mobility that few of us are able to escape as the years increase.

The impact of the stereotypes

Why is it that so little is written about older women and that their lives are not thought to merit greater consideration? In our view it is the stereotypes of old age that discourage people from examining the elderly: old age is too depressing to consider. This in turn blocks any possibility of learning anything about old age before we reach it, of taking steps to try and ensure that the quality of our lives is at least maintained at that stage. In a recent book, Cynthia Rich relates an instance that demonstrates this point. She had gone to buy a copy of a book entitled *The Social World of Old Women*. She writes:

When I was standing in line to buy this book, a woman behind me, possibly in her mid fifties, stared at the cover and asked eagerly 'Is that a good book?' And then, immediately afterwards, 'It's not depressing is it?'

This attitude and refusal to look enables Barbara MacDonald to say about America in 1983:

'Today I walk into New Words Bookstore in Cambridge and see the shelves filled, and realise that, with a few exceptions, our lives are not recorded there, only half our lives are there – our childhoods, our youths, our forties. The last half of our lives is unknown.[4]

By not looking we are also prevented from understanding and alleviating the more painful experiences of those who are currently old. There are important issues to look at here. How accurate are the views held about the elderly? If their lives are indeed limited, unfulfilling and frustrating, why is this the case? In what ways does society create and reinforce these experiences and how might they be changed? How successful are older people in confronting the prejudice they face and in shaping lives that they find satisfying?

Where studies do occur they tend to be focused upon specific problems experienced by the old. This emphasis has increased with the growing need to develop and expand social policies for the provision of care for old people. Such an emphasis is of course an important and legitimate area of concern: old people can find it difficult to look after themselves, and increasingly need to rely on others – be they family, friends or the welfare services. The danger comes when that is the only perspective on old age that we consider. Then we have only a partial view, one that ignores other aspects of the lives of particular individuals and of the elderly as a group. If no one completes the picture, this emphasis grows, making it easier to think of the elderly in this one-dimensional way, and to accept the picture of them as problematic, demanding and unreasonable.

4

This then reinforces the low esteem in which the elderly are held. Because women form the largest proportion of the very old, where the most severe problems of care are concentrated, the notion of elderly women as problematic becomes even more pronounced and generalised. What is necessary is a counter-balance to the problem-centred stance, an approach that draws out a more holistic picture of their lives by focusing upon the routine daily round, the everyday taken-for-granted, and which charts the fears, achievement, problems and pleasures of being an older woman.

The aims of this book

For all these reasons we set out to uncover and report upon the lives of older women, concentrating upon a more complete account of their thoughts, feelings and activities. We became interested in the lives of older women because we were involved in visiting them, either as part of volunteer schemes or as neighbours and friends. The book does not have its roots in an academic project or formal research discussions, but in the fact that we enjoyed visiting, talking and listening to older women, and found them interesting. We simply became curious enough about some of the things they said, and the way they organised their lives, to want to find out more.

We wanted to obtain personal accounts of the lives of a group of women, presenting them in the women's own words. We tried to ensure that the women talked about the topics they thought important, rather than being guided along certain paths by us. The interviews are therefore relatively unstructured. Other approaches (for example, pre-selecting issues to be considered) might well have produced a neater, more orderly set of accounts, but only at the risk that our own views about what was important would have dominated. This does not mean that we lack views or comments about what the interviews reveal, but we have deliberately tried to separate our comments from the interviews, and to express them only in the introductions and the final chapter.

Understanding the lives of older women

Subjective accounts of the lives of older women are an important first step. On their own, however, they do not take us far enough. There remains the question of how to make sense of their lives, how to interpret what they tell us.

As we have seen, one of the reasons why old age is regarded as uninteresting and restricted is that we find it very difficult not to continue to judge people in terms of the prevalent 'productive' norms of western society. To be successful in such a society means that one must constantly strive to achieve, and must develop wider and more expansive horizons. Judged by these values the lives of older people will frequently appear diminished, possibly even failures. Their obviously productive role has gone with their loss of employment; in addition, for women, their value in supporting other people – looking after children, partners or elderly relatives – may cease as children leave home and parents or partners die. What is needed is an alternative way of interpreting old age, a different framework in which to understand and respect the goals of older people; one that does not always contain an implicit comparison with earlier goals. This is one of the things that we hope to achieve from this book. Such an alternative framework would recognise, for example, that pleasure comes not from 'achievement', but from friendship in the coffee shop, a holiday among those with the same interests, a course undertaken for its own sake rather than as a means to subsequent use or gain. In short, the chance to be valued as a person rather than a producer. These goals may appear limited – in fact they are simply different. The reality of entering the last phase of life is that the set of values that guides the thinking of older people undergoes a fundamental change.

However, while values may alter in old age, what continues

and is much harder to change is, first, the structural poverty and dependence that women experience, and, second, the power of stereotypes that create a pervasive ageism in society. Growing older can therefore be a painful and frustrating experience: the chance to achieve contentment and fulfilment is continually thwarted and challenged so that loneliness, isolation and anxiety are never far away, and are periodically overwhelming.

Economic resources remain a source of power and status within our society. Older people, and particularly women, who form the larger part of the elderly population, have lower incomes and less economic power than other groups in society. This is both a reflection of the low status accorded to them, and a major cause of restrictions on the quality of their lives, affecting not only the range of activities they can undertake, but also basic conditions of housing and heating.

One of the most obvious problems faced by the elderly is diminished physical strength and mobility. The combination of stiffening joints and slippery pavements brings a fear of falling that keeps many people at home during the winter. Many face more serious medical conditions that at best sap their energy, and at worst need frequent attention. Declining physical health increases the extent to which people have to ask for help, and their sense of dependence where they cannot reciprocate.

Less obvious are the social attitudes and structures that limit the lives of older women, and often trap them in positions of disadvantage. These attitudes and expectations are frequently long-standing and internalised, and supported by a lengthy socialisation process. The emphasis within society upon 'the couple' as the appropriate social unit often results in women losing contact with their friends when they marry, leaving them dependent upon the family for support and friendship. The extent to which widows and single women can develop a social life is restricted. For married women the traditional family structures and routines of socialisation establish patterns of obligations and expectations that they continue to meet even in circumstances of declining health. At the same time, norms that identify women as the providers of services

7

may make it difficult for them to request help from those for whom they generally provide, while those generally in receipt of services from women may find it difficult to regard such requests as legitimate, regarding them as unreasonable and unnecessary.

The lives of older women thus remain heavily dependent on the definitions and resources that are made available to them by the rest of society. It is within this framework that the majority of older women strive to achieve the contentment and pleasure they so value.

The extent to which they recognise the forces shaping their lives varies considerably. Many women now over 60 have been denied opportunities in both education and work, thus limiting their potential for independence. They remain unconnected to and untouched by the activities of the women's movement, which in turn has directed little attention to older women. Their socialisation has been towards the traditional patterns of marriage and family and a dependent role within that framework. This is not to say that marriage and family were not deliberate choices – indeed, many who did not marry or have children regard it as a matter of regret. However, the power of socialisation and the resulting absence of a critique on the part of many women does not make their position legitimate, justify the attitudes of others to them, or make structural inequalities acceptable. Rather, it points to the need to consider how change might be achieved, and how likely it is that older women are in a position to secure such change.

Even when women do recognise that their position is a consequence of wider social structures they are often at a point in their lives where their capacity to secure change is at its lowest. It is often only when women reach old age and begin to reflect on their lives that they question some of their earlier decisions that now affect their present position – precisely when their resources, strength and networks are all most limited. In any case it is vital to remember that almost all older women today have to rely for their social and physical survival upon kin or those providing welfare services for many aspects of their lives. Even where the dependency is recognised, and women feel that they are treated harshly by those around them, it is hard to bite the hand that feeds.

These points have important implications for what we might learn from a book like this. The experiences of old age are in fact mapped out at a much younger age and it is here that we need to begin to set the scene for a happier old age. We need to work to challenge some of the structures and attitudes that later constrain and limit us: the pressure to conduct social life in terms of a couple, for example; an inadequate income; attitudes towards old age that make it difficult for the elderly to ask for and be granted respect, and treatment that accords them dignity and recognition. Younger women should also examine the extent to which they can offer support to older women, either in terms of friendship or by providing them with an opportunity to contribute to our lives. Mrs Pullan, a woman interviewed in this book, has found her retirement particularly difficult and lonely. But one period stands out for her as different and satisfying. This was when by chance some young women came to live next door to her, several of them not yet employed. They offered each other companionship, looked forward to seeing each other, and as Mrs Pullan says, 'For a while my life was so different . . . We helped each other quite a lot.' But this companionship was lost when Mrs Pullan moved.

One response to some of the needs of old age – for example, friendship, respect and mutual support – might be to seek to establish new patterns of living and sharing that move away from the conventional arrangements of hierarchy, exploitation and productivity found in society. There appear to be few such developments as yet amongst the current generations of older women. Some women establish a home together, but frequently this is brought about by economic necessity and the desire for companionship rather than through a rejection of conventional norms and a search for a different way of life. Such models of living may, however, become more prominent with subsequent generations whose members have as younger women challenged the dominant forms of social organisation.

9

Interviewing older women

Having decided to pursue our interest in the lives of older women, we had to consider how to obtain the information and who to talk to. As we have explained earlier, we wanted the women to talk about their lives, with the minimum of prompting or input from us. We adopted the administrative notion of 'retired' or 'old' as beginning at 60, and recorded a series of conversations with 14 women whose ages ranged from 60 to 90. Both of us knew older women we thought would be willing to participate, and other names were suggested to us by them, by friends, and by social and community workers in the area. We wanted to talk to women in a number of different situations: women who had been, or were still in paid employment; women who had never worked outside the home; single, married and widowed women, immigrant women. The women interviewed are not intended to be in any way special but just ordinary women living their lives, organising and arranging their activities in the ways they can or wish, who were willing to talk about themselves and their current lives. They were all living in the East Midlands at the time of the interviews. In presenting the interviews we have used a variety of styles; some are short, some longer; some narrative, others in a question-and-answer form. Some chapters introduce one person and others more than one. Where a chapter brings women together, this is either because they were interviewed together, or because it highlights differences and similarities between women where too often it is assumed that they will have common experiences. All the women were visited several times and the interviews were recorded. Most of the women we approached were keen to talk; just a few felt unable to. One lived in an old people's home: she was obviously very unhappy with certain aspects of the care and may have feared reprisals if she made criticisms. Some Asian families were also unhappy about our interviewing their female relatives on their own.

Talking to older women raised some interesting questions as well as problems for us as interviewers. For many reasons, older women are accessible, in the sense that they are generally willing to help and, once familiar with the idea of being asked, are keen to talk. Most of them (but not all by any means) have time and enjoy visits and additional company. Undoubtedly some felt flattered, or at least pleased to be the centre of attention, particularly where they felt strongly that older people were undervalued by society. Others, as the interviews show, had had lifetimes of holding back their views because of social situations in which they were subordinates often where their views had always been assumed to coincide with those of either their husbands or other household members.

The women are referred to in different ways in the interviews. Sometimes as Miss or Mrs, sometimes by their Christian names. Fictitious names have been used throughout although the form of address used by the women themselves when we first met them has been retained. Indeed, none of the women ever changed the way they wished to be addressed as we came to know them better.

There is a growing literature in the area of women's studies that discusses the question of the accessibility of women to researchers and the relevance of traditional research stances (see for example Roberts and Bell, *Doing Feminist Research*[5]). One theme in the literature concerns the different responses of women to male as opposed to female researchers. Finch[6] describes the greater willingness of women to trust other women, to confide, and to provide information that would not be available to male interviewers. Such trust is argued to be based upon the respondent's identification of the interviewer as a woman, someone who shares a similar structural position and is subject to the same cultural expectations as the interviewer. Such an approach requires the researcher to adopt a shared or non-hierarchical role and to develop trust by a willingness to share experiences and to enter into discussion. This approach provides a further basis for empathy and increases the interviewee's confidence in the researcher. Oakley[7] notes that this kind of researcher participation is particularly frowned upon in methods textbooks, which provide guidelines about how to

11

avoid answering questions and how to maintain social distance. By contrast, Oakley argues for exchange and participation, partly on the ideological grounds of offering support to other women, but also as an essential prerequisite for establishing trust and enabling the researchers to uncover and understand more accurately the respondents' experiences and perceptions of social processes. For writers such as Oakley this involvement does not jeopardise the quality of the data or subsequent analysis, but rather enhances it:

> The mythology of 'hygienic research' with its accompanying mystification of the researcher and the researched as objective instruments of data production must be replaced by a recognition that personal involvement is more than dangerous bias – it is the condition under which people come to know each other, and to admit others into their lives.[8]

Our experience of interviewing women was equally one of recognising the willingness of other women to talk and confide – in fact an overwhelming sense of ease in talking to women. The very act of asking them to talk, and our interest in their activities, was a source of amazement to most of them, but also a sign to them that they mattered in their own right and were thought to do so by other women. There was clearly identification with us as women. 'You know as well as me what they're like,' said one lady, referring to her husband. 'You had so many more opportunities than we had.' 'I wasn't allowed to do what you've been able to do,' said another, assuming a shared knowledge and understanding of traditional attitudes towards women. We often exchanged views and experiences. The shared role of women allowed the women to confide and discuss particularly sensitive issues – most notably the loss of husbands, parents and children.

Some aspects of our interviews with older women were, however, problematic, even given the trust and basic feeling of ease. A number had to struggle hard to express their ideas and feelings, especially in the early stages of a meeting. For many the activity of speaking some thoughts aloud was relatively new. Some lacked the vocabulary to develop their ideas: 'Oh, how can I say it . . . what I'm trying to get at is . . . you know.' In addition, many of these women have lived with – and accepted – strongly developed conventions about what can be spoken aloud and how ideas can be expressed. A number knew they thought one thing and generally said another, and had done so for years. As some of the interviews progressed some of the women indicated they had just told us something they had never told anyone before. In one case it concerned the way the woman had been treated by her employer. In another, a woman explained how she had thought about leaving her husband 20 years ago but had never said anything to him or anyone else until now. Long-established conventions that preclude the discussion of sexual matters remain quite strong amongst these older women, not only with regard to their own lives, but when commenting on other people and other activities. Speaking of how little television she watched one said, 'It's not right – there's too much of it, you know, the sex bits. I'm often embarrassed when my son-in-law is here, I try and turn it off before they come.' Such reticence was a characteristic of all the women, but was particularly pronounced among those who had been in a dependent marital relationship and had never been in paid employment. This reticence is part of the socialisation process that these women experienced that has made it difficult for them to speak out.

Actual age is not a good guide to the general health, mobility, patterns of activity or attitudes of older women. This is often recognised in the discussions of the elderly by the use of characterisations such as the 'young old' and the 'old old' that are not solely age-related categories. In one area, however, years did appear significant for our interviewees in that it was the older women who had the greatest tendency to be repetitive and to focus their attention more firmly on the past. Their present was more 'getting by', 'passing time' or 'thinking about the past'. One woman in an old people's home simply said, 'What else is there to do? But anyway, those are the times I want to remember, when my husband was alive.'

Repetitiveness is difficult to handle in unstructured interviews, especially over several different visits, and we have edited where necessary. Another problem was that of failing memory. For some it was only an issue of dates or of who had been present at particular events, but for one or two it was a more serious matter, made more difficult by their own recognition of the problem and their struggles to contain it. The interviews could be quite stressful for these women. Where such problems did occur it was usually in relation to details, and all these women continued to care for themselves at home. However, older people who sometimes forget things often appear less capable, and if they seem to be vague others may step in, so they may well lose control over decisions or in making plans for themselves. As one interviewee said, in relation to relief care in an old people's home, 'I don't know where it is, someone will let me know when to go and they will come and take me there.' Equally, failing memory amongst those still caring for themselves can place them in real danger.

The general issues discussed so far in this chapter form the backcloth against which we can set the accounts of everyday life provided by the women we spoke to. By reproducing these interviews we hope to share and make accessible the lives of those who are too easily forgotten. In so doing, one of the things that becomes apparent is the hidden courage displayed by these women in the face of ageism. These accounts teach us something about the challenge of old age, a challenge that could well be lessened through greater awareness by younger women of what lies ahead.

The trouble is that old age is not interesting until one gets there, a foreign country with an unknown language to the young and even the middle-aged. I wish now that I had found out more about it.[9]

2
Mrs Wates

Introduction

At 79, Mrs Wates was one of the older women we interviewed. Like a number of the other women she had certainly not thought of herself as old throughout her sixties, and she had been in paid and then voluntary employment until she was 72. Only recently had she become particularly conscious of her age, and so had begun to think about and see herself as old. It was the death of a close family member that had forced this recognition. People experience loss throughout their lives, but loss in old age does have some special characteristics. Quite simply it occurs more often, and from an already diminished circle takes away yet another of those who provide care, support and friendship with little likelihood that they will be replaced. Often such friendships are based on many years of shared experiences, and several of the women, including Mrs Wates, said that they had never envisaged being without those people. New friends, if they can be found, cannot provide the same sense of certainty and reassurance. The loss of Mrs Wates' sister triggered her thinking about the future and, as she acknowledged, focused her thoughts upon herself, revealing her own fears and increasing her sense of anxiety and inadequacy. When we talked to her she returned again and again to her dread of being left alone as a result of her husband dying first. On a practical level, she was frightened that she wouldn't know what to do, either on his death, or with their affairs afterwards; emotionally, she feared loneliness in a world where almost all those whom she knew, loved and felt comfortable with and who loved her, had gone.

The interview shows very clearly the way in which Mrs Wates designed a daily routine to help allay such fears and to guard against the isolation and loneliness that she already felt to some extent and knew would get worse. She deliberately keeps contact with as many people as possible and joins everything she can. The activity isn't really important, what does matter is the opportunity to meet with and talk to others.

Mrs Wates was born in a village outside Nottingham in 1905. She left the village school at 12 and went to a city school and then on to secretarial college. She completed the twelve-month course in shorthand, typing and bookkeeping in nine months, and started working for a firm in the Lace Market area of the city. When she was 24 she married. Her fiancé was the village schoolteacher and they met at the local tennis club. He moved into the police force in order to be able to marry. They spent 30 years in Birmingham, bringing up two children, and then on her husband's retirement they moved to the south coast. Mr Wates is now in his eighties. Five years ago they returned to the village of her birth. They rent an end-of-terrace house that has no garden and is approached via an entry passage.

When you decided to leave the south, and came back here, how did you find somewhere to live?

My sister found it. We'd only been here a year when she died. It was the biggest shock of my life because but for her I don't think we'd have come back. She found us this place. To be truthful, I don't like it, still we've got it, but you see I can't see anybody and I'd like to. I've no windows on to the street and no garden. Now my husband, he's satisfied here. I'd rather be where I can see people, but you can't get anywhere today can you? We just looked at this one house because there weren't any more. It was ever such a job to get this one. We rent this house. That's my landlord next door, in the garden. To be frank we've never had any money to buy a house. Not when you're educating your children to such an extent. I know I went to work but . . . I think the top and bottom of it is that I've been too generous in my life to one and another. My sister always said, 'You're too generous, you'll never have any money.' I wouldn't think of going to any place, or asking anyone to take me but what I paid. Still I'm here. I'm 79, I've enjoyed life.

Do you regret being so generous?

Now and again. I can see what a fool I've been. I could have had more for myself. But perhaps not as happy. What's money? You find it out as you get older. I know it's nice and you wish you'd got more, but . . . I really came back because of my sister. She'd married someone in the village, but I'd always wanted to be back near her.

Did you still have a lot of friends here?

No, it was really just my sister. But there are a lot of people I know from years ago. Gradually I've found them all out. Several of them have died, but I've got quite a lot of people I knew here. I'd not kept contact with them, but they say, 'Oh – Audrey Pie,' that's my maiden name. I don't usually know them from Adam, but they know me and remember me which is a good thing perhaps because I'm able to talk to them. I don't think I go out now once but what I meet somebody. They all call me Audrey and half of them don't know my married name.

Do you think of yourself as a 'pensioner', as being old?

I do now. Being old depends on how you feel from day to day, how fit you are. My sister dying brought it all nearer.

How long ago did that happen?

Let's see, how long . . . you see time passes more quickly when you get older. I find that. She was 72 and I'm 79. There were

17

three years between us, so she'd be 76 now. So that's four years ago that she died. It had a tremendous effect because she was my only sister. I lost my brother when he was 49, so there was only she and I. We always got on well together and we were very close so it was a bit of a shock when she died. We used to see each other every day and share things. I never thought she would, never, perhaps because she was younger than me. It just shows you doesn't it? I just had to go on as usual, it was all I could do, so that's what we do. But I miss her so much – still. But as well, just lately since my legs have got so bad I've realised I'm much older. But I get about all I possibly can. I mean, you've got to take each day as it comes and what will be will be. Each day as it comes. Some days you're fitter than others as you get older. I'm lucky that I've only these bad legs, and they were only brought on through falls. I fell down some hotel steps and they bandaged the leg so tight that you can see the marks still. That's eight years ago. Then I broke both my wrists tripping in a shop, and I've also broken my humerus, is that it, and the ball and socket was out. I went to the medical centre and general hospital for physiotherapy for nearly a year, but what's done me more good than anything is going to keep-fit on a Thursday and I've got my arm up now. I couldn't before.

Tell me about how you spend your day.

Well I'll tell you, I've been awake since four o'clock this morning. I always wake early. I lie till about quarter past five and then I come down and make a cup of tea and probably write a letter, and listen to the forecast at five to six. Then I go back up to bed for a while and get up about half past seven to eight and just take my time. I get my husband up about half eight and we have breakfast at nine o'clock. If I've any shopping to do – well, before that there are the beds to do and I have a dust around. It just depends which week Susan's coming. She helps me in the house and turns out. She can move things I can't. My husband nearly always cooks the dinner in the pressure cooker because I won't touch the thing. I don't like it, I'm frightened of it. A friend of mine had a pressure cooker and it went wrong and tripe was stuck on the ceiling. Ever since then I've never touched it. But he's always used it. He does most of the cooking now.

Do you go out very much?

Yes, nearly every afternoon. I try and get out for a walk, even if it's only round the block. I go to the library. I read a lot of library books. This is one I've got. I have to have something light, and something I can see. This one is in big print because I read in bed when I wake. I like nurses' books. I read a lot of these; *The New Pupil Midwife*. It's not bad, I can manage that. Some afternoons I go to the clubs, or the café for a cup of tea or an ice and I meet Peggie and we go to the coffee shop. I look forward to going out. I go out a lot, but I have to consider my husband as well. He doesn't come with me. He won't go out to meet, sort of thing. He'll go to the library occasionally, but he counts his bowls as his exercise. They play outside in the summer and indoors in the winter in Nottingham. He reads an awful lot, mind, he's one of the best! You see I like company and I miss it if I'm not amongst it. That's why now I join everything I can: Women's Institute, Mothers' Union, various things, anything. Like others I know, they're lonely too, that's why we all join.

How do you spend the evenings?

I like quizzes on T V. I don't like the murders and shooting, no wonder there's so much crime. What's that programme with Compo, I like that, *Last of the Summer Wine*. I've been there. I've got a picture, here look [and she pulled it out from under the table], Nora Batty's cottage. I really like that. I don't watch too much, I fall asleep, that's my trouble.

What about in the winter?

Oh I get bored stiff then, having to stay in all the time. Because I'm frightened of falling then you see. But I go out then when I possibly can. I've got an orthopaedic walking-stick. I dread the winter. I go out some nights, a lady collects me and takes me to play solo and brings me back. At night my husband and I play cards or scrabble. We haven't done lately but we shall have to start now the winter's coming. He's been bowling at night you see, and I go sometimes and watch. That's where he is this afternoon. But even though I've got friends here now, they don't pop in because, well, it's simply that I've got a husband and they haven't, quite a lot of them. They're nearly all widows and they won't come. Queer isn't it? I don't know why they won't come. You see we've only got this one room, and you know what women are; they like to talk. That's why they won't come, I think. Tomorrow afternoon I'm going to play bridge with some friends. I like the cards, and you have to think and that keeps me active. We go to one another's houses on a Saturday afternoon. Monday I go to the launderette with the washing and in the afternoon I go to the library or have a walk and I do the ironing in the evening. Tuesday I just do bits and bobs and then go to Ladies Circle. I take that quite often. At night I do the odd job or two, but more often than not I fall asleep I'm so tired. Wednesday's coffee morning, and there's the Over 60's in the winter.

Do you ever talk about the future, or think about it?

Oh yes, we have to do, talk about . . . but I'm afraid of dying. Only yesterday I said to him, 'You'll have to make a list of our assets, the few that we've got,' so he did. I don't know what to do, I've no more idea than fly. You've got to think of that sort of thing at 80 and 79 but I don't like doing it. I know the first thing to do is ring the doctor. Oh, it will come naturally. God will help me. But, I'm hoping to go before him. Sounds a bit selfish doesn't it, but I don't want to be on my own. I should have to do it if that was the way it worked out, I should have to get used to it the same as other people, but I mean, I'd hope to get out of this place into a council place if anything happened to him. We'd go now if we could, but they're not to be got, you know. I'd like a bungalow, but it's hopeless. You never know, one might come out of the blue. I'm afraid that I might be left on my own. I'd be lonely. I know what I'd do, I'd go out all the while, be with other people. But then if my legs give way I can't. But surely somebody will come and help. He knows I'm afraid. He says I'm silly, really. What he says is what is to be will be. But you do, when you get older you think of these things. My sister going really brought it home. I've thought of it ever since. Of course people are living so much older these days aren't they?

Have you made plans about what you'd do if you were on your own?

No, I don't know, I don't like to think about it. I'd have to stay here until I could get somewhere else. I know I wouldn't go and live with my children. I don't think it's right. I don't, because young ones don't agree always with elderly people. Their ideas are not your ideas. I suppose if I was ill and couldn't look after myself I'd have to go, but I wouldn't go willingly. It wouldn't be fair to them, and I wouldn't like it. No I wouldn't, 'specially with my daughter. She's got typical views of her own, and you can't persuade her different. Awkward, and you can't alter her. She's just been away. I shall have to ring on Sunday, I generally do, and see how she's getting on. She never rings me. Of course she's at work three days a week, she does the accounts. Then she's got her housework to do and the dinners to cook, so she's not much time for writing has she? She could phone, but I suppose she wants to sit down sometimes. My granddaughter writes so she tells me.

When you wake early in the morning what do you do and think about?

All sorts of things. Worry. I've no need to worry, I suppose, but you do. Why hasn't so-and-so-written? Why haven't I heard from my daughter? She seldom writes or rings up but she says that if she wasn't all right we'd soon know, but I still worry. My granddaughter writes. I'm the one that likes to correspond, but the youngsters have different ideas altogether. I've always worried. I'm a proper worrier. My husband says he's never known anyone able to worry so much over nothing.

I think about what might happen to me. I'm frightened I'll be left alone. 'What have you got to worry about,' he says. 'You won't starve if I die.' I'd still get the police pension as well as the state one. I'm all right in that respect, but it's just the thought of being without him. That's why I hope I go first. I'm not very good in the nights. It's worse then. I hate the dark. I never sleep with the curtains drawn. I'm frightened. I always think of myself in a coffin. I know it's silly but I do. I have to take sleeping tablets, every night, but I still wake at four. I've had them for quite a while. When I wake my brain's all of a whirl, always working, even when I'm in bed. My husband can make his mind a blank, but I can't. I think, think, think, and of course in the night things mount up. It's funny, but you can only think of the bad things then, not the good times.

How do you think that most other people regard the elderly?

Well [a long pause], some do and some don't. Some have no time for you and others are all right. I find when I go out, I stand on the corner of the main street ages trying to cross. Lots of people ignore me and don't help, but there's always someone in the end who offers to take me across. They've seen me standing there. But those youngsters. They'll throw a bike down in front of you on the pavement. I make them pick them up. I don't feel written off though. I go to Keep Fit with Peggie, and much younger ones than I go, and they don't take any notice of us in a nasty way. They don't poke fun. They know we do what we can. We go on the outings and there's some younger people there, but usually we're all of an age and that makes it better I think. But the youngsters don't really bother me. I'm more afraid of falling when I'm out than of anything. We go on holidays from here too. It's better than going on our own. Everything's arranged for you. You're not lumbered with your luggage. We couldn't manage ours. Things are arranged so we like to go with a party. I'm about the eldest. We've just had a good week in Torquay. It was a very nice hotel and lots to do.

3
Mrs Ruby Harman

Introduction

Ruby lives alone in a semi-detached house in a quiet end of an estate of privately-owned middle-range houses. She is a small, well-dressed, neat woman, who gives the appearance of strength and energy despite her small frame. She is still married, although her husband left her about 13 years before, when she was 60, to live with a younger woman. He owns and maintains the house. Ruby moved here from the other side of town about two years ago, partly because the house was smaller and easier to run and partly to be nearer her son and daughter-in-law.

Ruby found the desertion of her husband very difficult to accept. She is obviously still torn between feelings of great regret and great anger. Her response to the separation has been to adopt an approach that will bring her least confrontation. She prefers her ambiguous legal position to going to court either for a divorce or to secure property or maintenance rights. Similarly, she doesn't openly question or obstruct Frank's visits to her, although she sometimes finds them pointless and annoying. Those who have been influenced by or have grown up with the thinking of the women's rights movement may well feel that Ruby ought to be more assertive in guarding her own interests. However, it is important to see that this separation from her husband has been only one of a number of major family crises that Ruby has had to face throughout her life. First, her father did not return from service in the First World War. He was 'reported missing, assumed dead' when Ruby was only a small child. Then during the Second World War Ruby's husband was away for five years, leaving Ruby to bring up her two sons on her own. Jim, the younger of these two sons, emigrated shortly after he married, but his wife and baby were killed in a car crash. He returned to England with his son, Bill. Ruby gave up her job to care for her grandchild, although Bill eventually went to live with his maternal aunt. Some years later Jim remarried, but shortly afterwards died of cancer, leaving Bill an orphan. Even this tragedy was compounded by quarrels and legal action over the care and custody of Bill; quarrels that Ruby did not invite but which greatly affected her. Like many people in their seventies Ruby has also seen the death of her near relatives, her sister, her cousins, her aunts and uncles, so she feels very much bereft of her own generation.

It would be easy to allow such tragedies to make you bitter and angry. To avoid that, Ruby has adopted an attitude of stoicism and outward acceptance. It is important to her that she should try to continue in an organised way, and maintain her position by appearing to put things behind her. By learning to cope with a series of misfortunes, Ruby seems to have developed a set of values that give prominence to appearances and respectability; values that say it is important not to break down in public, not to air your disappointments, or to discuss your personal affairs. This is in total contrast to her private pain, sorrow and disappointment. However, she is emerging with greater independence and a growing confidence as a result of her involvement in activities associated with the members of the pensioners' club.

Ruby is now 73, but she still works three mornings a week helping in the home of a retired couple. This couple are both considerably younger than Mrs Harman, but are not in good health. Ruby has been in some form of employment for much of her life, and still maintains the habit of an early start to the day.

I'm an early riser, I always have been, right from a kid. I can't lie in bed – I take my teapot upstairs and I've usually got a cup of tea made by half past six to a quarter to seven. I can't stop in bed, it is awful isn't it and I don't go to bed that late really, but I always read and don't put the light out until about midnight. Sometimes I have worse nights than others, when I don't sleep, but still I don't lie in, even at weekends. I should be an awful invalid, I really would. And as for going to sleep in the daytime, I couldn't do that. As a child I couldn't stop in bed. I can remember there was just my mother and sister and me and I can hear my mother saying it now on a Sunday morning: 'Go to sleep, the church bells haven't started yet.' I don't sleep any more now I'm getting older. A lot say you sleep less. I've got into the habit of reading at night and that helps me sleep.

I like to get started early, besides I go out to work three mornings and I get picked up at nine o'clock, so I have to be ready by then. The rest of the week, if I go into town I usually go early, on the nine-thirty bus. But it is nice to be able to please yourself. You see I haven't got anyone coming in for meals, I haven't got to get anything ready or be waiting on anyone, so I do more or less please myself over meals and everything. Although you don't seem as if you want so much food – so as for doing a lot of cooking for myself, I just don't, but if I feel like a cup of coffee or a cup of tea I make it and have it. But I don't have any routine – although I usually meet my friend on Tuesdays and we have lunch in the pub – I think I got out of the routine during the war, because there was no routine during the war. I shouldn't like a well-ordered life like that, it wouldn't suit me.

I don't like stopping in during the day. I say to myself, 'Oh, go out while you've got the chance; you never know what's in front of you,' so I'll go into town, and to a club one afternoon, or for a walk, or to work in the garden.

But I don't go out at night – no, I stop at home every evening.

I won't go out in the dark – I'd be afraid. Once, a couple of years ago, I walked back from town about half past nine – but my friend said, 'You never ought to walk that way by yourself, it's lonely on that green belt bit.' I just told her, 'Oh, I'd walk on the other side and I should go and knock on somebody's door if anybody was after me.' I think that's what I'd do, something like that . . . it's not very nice and it never ought to be like that – but what can someone like me do about it. I think the older you get you do feel more nervous really, and I don't think it's because we've talked ourselves into it; I think there really is danger out there – when you hear what some of these youths do, snatching handbags and all that. Then when that lady down the road was beaten up recently, that frightened everybody – I know that's over and done with now, but it still makes you wonder about things. Good Lord, when I was young I would walk home from anywhere in the dark, but I won't dare do that now, no more dare do it than fly. Once you start to think you're afraid then it's not worth it. I suppose being on your own makes it worse. So I stay in by myself in the evening – unless my son picks me up and brings me home. But you still have to come back to an empty house and I don't like that.

Well, I don't mind being on my own and I can pick what I want on the television – I don't mind – it does get you down a bit perhaps; it's loneliness, I suppose. Sometimes you wish you'd got somebody here, but it's one of those things, I haven't so I have to put up with it.

Sometimes when I'm on my own in the evenings, I think if Frank was still here I wouldn't have to be on my own . . . that makes me sad in a way, but mad as well . . . Sometimes I get so cross – I think I had all the rough time, the hard times; I had five and a half years on my own during the war when he was in the forces and I had to bring the children up on my own, with no money: we'd got hardly anything in those days. Then we had the years in the newsagents, getting up at five o'clock every morning – I sometimes think it's a pity 'she' didn't meet him when we were in the bloomin' newsagents. If she had had to get up at five in the morning, I wonder if that would have cured her. I think it would. After all those years together, I sometimes think I deserved a bit more, and now she's reaping all the benefits. Still, there you are, that's life isn't it. It doesn't bother me so much now, but it took me five years really to accept it . . . At first I never told a soul – even my next-door neighbour who was a good friend, she didn't know he'd gone for over a fortnight . . . it's because you feel so guilty that you don't tell people. You're not the guilty one and it's wrong to feel guilty, but you do . . . It took me about five years to really accept what had happened . . . till in the end I began to think he's just not worth it – he's not worth that much and I'm not going to worry over him.

He just left one night. When I got home one teatime there was a note from him – he'd left and he has never come back. I knew he had been seeing this other woman, night after night, and I told him I was fed up with it. Mind you, we never talked about her and have never talked about her since – not even mentioned her – I just assume he is still with her, but I don't know. I don't even know where he lives. I don't have his address, although I do have his phone number now. Not that I would ever phone him, but I was given it when our son Jim was so very ill. I saw him a lot when Jim was ill – he was very good over that; he took me to London several times, so I could visit him, and we went together to the funeral – yes, he was very good then, but I think it is because he feels guilty. He feels very, very guilty. Since Jim died he comes to visit me regularly – about once a week, I suppose. I sometimes feel as though I don't know what to talk about when he comes. He talks on about people we used to know and that – but he never mentions 'her', he never even says 'we' when he talks about places he's been. I don't know what to think about his visits but I just go along with it.

He did ask me for a divorce, right at the beginning; I said no – I said to him, I meant what I said when I took my vows when we got married. He's never asked me again since that – so we're still married really. We've got nothing legal about being separated – but even so he's always been fair about money – he still owns this house – that doesn't worry me. I just let him get on with it. Once he tried to explain to me about his will and that, but I only listened with half an ear, because the whole situation makes me so cross at times. Yet I know it's no use being like that, because you're only punishing yourself – you just get bitter and nasty and that's no good as it makes things no better. But Frank has been fair about money, he gives me something every week, although the solicitor once said that I ought to be getting more, but I'm not bothered really. If I'm careful I can manage. I know this is his house, but I'm not worried about that. I'll go on living here, but if it came to it and if, say, I couldn't manage here on my own – if something happened to me and I couldn't get up or down the stairs, for instance – then I'd have to move. But if I did that and this house was sold, then he has always said if that happened then I'd get half the money. Of course, I want to stay here, but if the time should come and I couldn't manage on my own then I'm on a housing list. I had the chance of a flat last year, but of course I didn't want it – so I've gone on a deferred list. I shouldn't want to go into a flat – it doesn't appeal to me at all – well, it's not your own is it? Not like here where I can go outside if I want and I've got my bit of garden – I've heard such awful things about the flats, I shouldn't want to go, not until I've got to. But you never know, anything could happen. Just the other day my friend who also lives on her own said to me, 'What would I do supposing I couldn't get out of bed in the morning?' I said to her, 'Oh, don't think about anything like that.' But sometimes you do think about it and wonder what would you do if you were taken ill. Well you just don't have to think about things like that, because you'd scare yourself to death, so I don't let myself think about it – no I don't – no way. Yet if you are a bit low and depressed these things do go through your mind; you could worry yourself sick – so I'm determined I'm not going to think about it.

You see, while I'm still as fit as I am now, I'm not too worried, and I try to get out and about as much as I can. That's one reason why I've kept on working. I still do three mornings a week, which can be quite a lot. Sometimes I get tired and wonder why I bother – but it helps to get me out of the house and it gives me that bit of extra money – it's that little bit extra that makes all the difference, and of course it's all mine. I always have to be a bit careful with money. I couldn't just order a taxi to take me out if I wanted, and I have to think twice about the bill before I use the phone. In the evening, if I'm a bit lonely I won't use the phone just to have a natter; I only use it when I need to make arrangements or something like that. I can manage all right on my money, it's just that I need to be careful and the bits I get from the Trings help me with holidays and extras like that. Not that I'd do the job just for the money – it's getting out as well. I told you I'm not a great one for sitting about all day, so it gives me something to do. The Trings want me to go more often and to prepare the meals, but I'm not going to do any extra – sometimes I think I'd like to do a bit less, but they want me to keep coming. Mr Tring comes for me in the car and brings me home – otherwise I wouldn't go. I sometimes think it's funny that they think they need help in the house now they are getting older, but you know I'm a good bit older than either of them – but they're not well and that's what makes the difference. So long as you have your health you can manage.

It's funny when you think about being old, I don't really see myself as old and I don't think my grandchildren see me as old. I think they see an old lady as someone bent over with a stick and hardly able to walk. That's how I remember my granny – she was an old granny to me for as long as I knew her – nowadays people stay looking younger for much longer. I suppose it's because they keep interested in clothes and fashions and that. I think we all pay more attention to our appearances than we used to. I go to the hairdressers every fortnight now – and I shall do so while I can. I like to keep myself smart although I don't change my style of clothes to follow fashion. No, I don't think of myself as old and I don't think people see me as being old. I mean people know roughly what age I am but they don't seem to think of me as old, and that's nice really. I think keeping yourself young has a lot to do with having gone out to work and having had to mix with all sorts of people – that keeps you up with things. Although nowadays I do enjoy being with people of my own age-group – you talk the same language as them, don't you? That's why I enjoy this club that I go to on a Tuesday – they are all retired, the folk that go there. Some of them think that I'm a widow and I don't always enlighten them, although I wouldn't like to know someone for long and deceive them like that – and anyway it doesn't bother me now, so I just say, 'I haven't got a husband.'

At this club we don't do a lot – have a cup of tea, maybe have a speaker and in the summer go for trips out, although I don't often go on those. One of the ladies who goes is a real live-wire and she organises these holidays staying in a hotel at the seaside, but usually out of season. I never used to go away like that, but this year I'm going twice. I went to Llandudno in May and I've booked to go away again in October. I worry a bit about the money, but then I think I may as well go while I can. Now I've been away once or twice I really enjoy it. It's good to have the company for a while, and it gives you something to look forward to. It's good to do different things, things you have never done before.

4
Mrs Hatter

Introduction

Mrs Hatter is nearly 90, small, and generally in good health, although slightly deaf in one ear. She lives in an old people's home. Approximately five per cent of the population over 65 in the United Kingdom live in some form of institution. In the East Midlands, the local authorities provide places in old people's homes for about 15 in every 1000 of those aged 65 and over. In addition, other people may regularly spend one or two days a week in such homes if day care is provided.

Mrs Hatter's home is purpose-built and run by the local authority. They take residents and day-care people, and both men and women. Downstairs there are offices, a kitchen, a large TV room and a dining-room. Large glass doors lead to a paved area where people can sit outside if the weather is fine, although the washing is also hung out in this area. Upstairs there are single bedsitting rooms, plus one or two small sitting-rooms each with armchairs and a television. One of these sitting-rooms belongs (unofficially) to Mrs Hatter and her friend Mrs Mullard, who is older and in poor health and, in Mrs Hatter's view, very depressed and 'a bit of a grumbler these days'. The two women tend to spend their time together there and few other residents intrude. The social worker calls to see them each week, and they really look forward to her visits.

Mrs Hatter talked to us in her bedroom. It was full of photos of her relations and mementos of her life with her husband.

All their married life was spent in the area, although Mrs Hatter was born and brought up in Yorkshire and retains a strong Yorkshire accent. She left school at 13 and trained as a milliner. Like one of our other interviewees (Mrs Foules), she was a good story-teller and loved the chance to recount the raids over Loughborough during the Second World War. Her ability to recount and reflect is not limited to the past. Mrs Hatter is equally reflective and perceptive about institutional life and the processing of the residents that occurred in the home. These insights enabled her to gain some room for manoeuvre.

Mrs Hatter openly admitted that she had regrets about coming to the home. She had lived previously with her family, with no apparent or overt tension, and as far as she could tell she had not caused them to alter their lives. Yet she sensed that her just being there was a difficulty, and so she felt uncomfortable and a bit in the way. In the end those feelings led to her accepting the suggestion that she should move to where she could be looked after, although she has never really understood why she had to leave.

Institutional living inevitably imposes some uniformity and routine upon the inhabitants. A lot of the life of the residents becomes public, with communal meals, sitting areas and discussions with the staff. Much of this irked Mrs Hatter and some of it she found undignified and embarrassing. She resented the lack of privacy: for example, staff could walk straight into her bedroom, or answer her questions and requests in public situations such as at meal times.

Mrs Hatter had established a routine and a territory in order to safeguard her privacy and control her life. She didn't challenge the institution openly, as she knew that there could be penalties for complaints, but she found other ways of preserving some independence. Every afternoon after lunch she went to her room, and the others knew not to disturb her. There she did bits of washing and mending and then 'sat and thought about the past'. She refused to go into the courtyard and wanted to distance herself from those she regarded as really old and pitiful. She deliberately kept herself to herself and mixed only with a few other residents: Mrs Mullard in the day, and a small group of three who watched television together and talked in the evening. The relationships with these women were kept formal. She never used first names, did not visit these women in their rooms, and, while they were companions, they were not confidantes.

I came here about four years ago but I wish I hadn't done so. Before that I lived with my son and his wife for about three years. I went there when my husband died. I'd been away in hospital for an operation on my eyes – I've had three operations for cataracts – and I was not long home when he died. I couldn't see too well but I managed to get help. It was an awful shock, he died of heart failure. After that my son said that on account of my eyes and the shock, that I couldn't stay in the bungalow on my own, so I went to live with him. We were comfortable enough, but, you know, you feel a bit in the way when they're young. I wasn't a lot of trouble. I never interfered with them, and they used to go out when they wanted and I never got lonely. I was all right, only it felt wrong sometimes, like I was a bit in the way. I used to go to Faringdon House on a Wednesday and I'd been to one or two other places for a fortnight while they'd been on their holidays. One time I'd been here. In the end they said I'd be better looked after, so when it was decided I'd move for good I said I'd come here, but I wish I hadn't done. I think it would have been better if I'd have gone to Faringdon House. Do you know it? There are one or two nice little places, better than here. Not so big and more friendly. Now if anyone asks me I always say that if you can keep your own home it's best to do so as long as possible because however nice a place is it's not like home is it? When you're at home you can do as you like, although when you get as you can't manage you've got to go somewhere like this. [She laughed.] You've no choice about being old. It's just one of those things you have to take. I don't think anyone wants to be old if they can't do for themselves, and there is such a lot like that now, they're really living too long.

I've not got many friends left, a lot of them have passed away but I have a cousin in Huddersfield. She's in a home. She's the last of the family apart from me. She'll be 84 this September. I write to her but I can't write a lot now because of my eyes. You do miss your friends really and so you have to think of the past. You sit and think about what happened because you haven't much future, have you?

Did you see in the paper where a woman was 105? She looked well, didn't she? I shouldn't want to live as long as that, though. I don't think anyone really wants to. As it is you spend most of your time thinking about the past, that's if you haven't dozed off! There is not much future to think about. I can't go on holidays now. We had some good ones in the past, but I never went abroad. My husband would not fly, he didn't like it at all so we never went.

Can you tell me how you spend your day?

What? . . . Oh yes, spend the day? Well, I get up by half past six, between six and half past, and of course it takes a bit longer getting dressed now, washing yourself and doing, than it used to. Then we have a cup of tea about seven, and they come and give you a tablet. It's a water tablet [she whispered, and grinned at me and laughed]. I don't need it but you have to take it from them so then I put mine down the sink. Breakfast is at half past eight. I usually go down there about eight o'clock with Mrs Mullard. She's not well now and she's become really depressed. We get a cup of tea around quarter past ten but I've already told them I won't bother this morning because I don't want them coming in. After breakfast you just have to sit and shut your eyes [she laughed]. I used to be able to crochet and do, and after dinner I come in here and either have a rest or rub through my hankies and do any bits of mending I've got. I do as much as I can. The others, them that can't, they have to do it for them. Later in the afternoon you just go and sit and perhaps talk, but Mrs Mullard doesn't talk much now. I do an awful lot of just sitting! They bring more tea and you can have a biscuit but then at half past five it's supper. That's what they call it but it's really tea. Later they bring you a milk drink, you can have what you want. But I tell you what: least said, best said about lots of things here. I watch television at night. Not up here, this one is no good and I go down to one of the rooms that has a colour one. There's only three of us so it's nice and quiet. I shouldn't want it on all day. I like a good film but not all that pop stuff and I'm not keen on Shakespeare. [There was a knock at the door and an attendant came in without waiting for a reply. He did not seem to have come in for any particular reason and looked around and went out again.] You see, that's the trouble with this place [she whispered]. Often they don't even knock. I told them not to come in today.

Are there people here who give you some company?

No. There's nobody much that you can really have a conversation with. They're all getting past it, same as some of them that's out there [Mrs Hatter pointed out of her window to the courtyard where several elderly people were sitting on benches]. They make them go outside whether they want to or not. I don't want to live to be crippled up. A lot of them here are turned 90 and there's all sorts, in wheelchairs as well, so I've something to be thankful for. I look forward to our visitor who comes on a Wednesday, she's very nice, and then of course I have my family and I go out occasionally. My niece fetches me sometimes for the day on a Sunday and it's a nice change, and nice food; a bit different from this place. A change all round and I love sitting in her garden.

I'm not really lonely here, but it is a big place. One real trouble is if you are down at the table it echoes and if anybody says anything, everybody can hear it. It's a big drawback I think, as you don't want everyone to hear what you've got to say. Say the matron or anyone comes and says something to you . . . well, everyone is looking and listening. Their eyes and ears are always on. That's the trouble in these big places. I really want somewhere private. The people here are always arguing, you know, and grumbling on one with another. I mean you don't find that in every place. Here, there are not enough staff to look after them all. As I am, I'm all right, but you never know how you're going to be. They're often busy and if you say you don't feel well often they won't take much notice. They won't call the doctor when you ask, they just give you an aspirin. Mind you, I never say anything because it could be worse.

I'll tell you what happened with my pension book. They have it here, they take it when you come in to help keep you and they give you so much back as spending money. I think they decide how much you get. In fact I do not know how much the pension is now. I've told them that they are to let me know when it's due again. It's nice to know. I know it belongs to me, but they have it. You never see the book. They never say anything to you about it. The spending money's not bad and if you don't want it they'll bank it for you. I've so many grand-children that as the birthdays come round I spend it. Odd times I go shopping too if I need a dress. Then my niece takes me so I need the money. I've told them they've got to let me know what I get.

Sometimes I cannot believe I'm 88 next month. I left school when I was 12 because my mother needed the help to look after my Grandma. Then at 13 I was apprenticed to millinery. You had to work 18 months for nothing, and then I went to another shop and got two-and-six a week. When I got married in 1920 we came to Loughborough. We went to London for a while but things weren't too rosy, so we came back by the Second World War . . . Listen that's the bell. I shall have to go dear, we get dinner now and I take a while to get down. I'm thankful I can do it on my own. I've got a walker that is a help some-times, especially getting up from old chairs and things. I never thought I'd get like this and this old, who'd have thought it?

5
Mrs Gandhi and Mrs Patel

Introduction

Over the last few decades the East Midlands has become home for many Asian families, in particular Asians who have come to this country from East Africa. By and large this group of immigrants are now well established and are often very successful in their chosen occupations. Many of these East African Asians came to Britain as refugees. The two women we interviewed were both from Kenya. The Asian communities in the East Midlands are now well established and support many of their own institutions and services.

Interviewing older Asian women raises problems over and above those discussed in our opening chapter. Two such problems are those of access and language. The children or grandchildren of several older women whom we had hoped to interview did not feel able to let us ask their mothers or grandmothers what they thought were personal questions. We could, perhaps, have reassured these families and overcome their reservations but we decided not to because we felt their immediate opinions should be respected.

Mrs Gandhi was interviewed through an interpreter; Mrs Patel spoke in English. Both methods produced complications, especially the latter. Mrs Patel did not find it easy to respond to questions that tended to be speculative or hypothetical, either about the future or about possible alternative choices in her past or present life. There are two likely explanations for this. First, she may have had difficulty in understanding the tense or grammar of a language in which she was not wholly fluent. Second, as we will see, both women had a sense of fatalism, of life being controlled by outside forces, that came over strongly in their conversation. We should be careful not to over-exaggerate this in relation to Asian women, for many of the women we interviewed had developed what amounted to codes of practice concerning topics of conversation that they thought appropriate or inappropriate for open discussion.

Despite these linguistic difficulties, Mrs Gandhi and Mrs Patel appeared extremely relaxed, open and welcome in receiving us, and very happy to talk. They are both in their sixties and came to England from East Africa with their husbands and children in the mid 1960s. The families came from Kenya as British passport holders, not as refugees. They came with many friends as part of an established community and were among the first Asian families to settle in the East Midlands. This seems to have contributed to a positive attitude to their experience of life in England. Certainly, Mrs Patel was highly optimistic about the acceptance of Asians within British society, an optimism that hasn't diminished despite her deep knowledge of the lives of many Asian families.

Both Mrs Gandhi and Mrs Patel have a husband and eight children still alive, as well as many grandchildren, most of whom live within easy reach of their mothers' homes. The native language of both women is Gujarati; Mrs Gandhi speaks no English, Mrs Patel's spoken English is good. Neither woman has ever learnt to read or write in any language.

Despite these common factors, the lives of these two women are in marked contrast to one another. Their very different experiences give the lie to any idea of a 'typical' Asian woman.

We knew very little about Mrs Gandhi before we met her. It came as something of a surprise to learn that she had left her husband within the past year and even more recently had become a practising Christian. She now lives alone in a small, very sparsely furnished flat in a new housing association development close to the centre of town. She is in reasonable health, although following a recent operation she has some difficulty in walking and uses a stick. She is extremely isolated in her flat – since her estrangement from her family she rarely has visitors. She was aware when making the decision to leave her husband that she was likely to lose contact with her old community and that making new friends or contacts outside that old community would be greatly inhibited by the language barrier. Despite the problems and the uncertain future she faces, Mrs Gandhi gives the impression of adopting a calm and thoughtful approach to life; a woman whose courage calls forth great admiration. At a time of life when women are becoming more dependent on their family, Mrs Gandhi deliberately removed herself from her home. By doing so she has found a happiness and a peace which she was unable to achieve within the family.

The conditions in Mrs Gandhi's flat are ideal for recording interviews on tape: quiet, uninterrupted, unhurried. None of these conditions could be said to operate in Mrs Patel's house. Here there is constant coming and going – daughters, cousins, workmen; lively grandchildren trying to gain the attention of 'Bah'; cups of tea and Indian snacks – not to mention the parrot who wanted to join in the conversation.

Mrs Patel lives with her husband and unmarried son in a terraced house in an older part of town, not far from the town centre. This house was given to them by their sons. Mrs Patel finds the maintenance of the house fairly strenuous and would prefer to move to a smaller, new house or flat. As she still wants to be near to the town centre this would mean a council flat. Her sons have not agreed to such a move because of the loss of social standing in moving from owner-occupation to a council property. This is not a pressing issue at present, but it is interesting to speculate whose will would be the stronger if Mrs Patel expressed her wish to move with more vigour.

Mrs Patel gives the impression of being a robust person, although she recognises that she is not as fit as she was. Unlike the younger generation, but like Mrs Gandhi, she wears a saree and has black, greying hair folded into a bun at the back. She is very obviously at the centre of her family – Mr Patel is still alive, but suffers from ill-health. She is an extremely lively and adventurous woman; an optimist whose life is guided by a strong religious belief. Perhaps it is from this that she derives her confidence and her purposeful approach to the future. Mrs Patel is a woman who laughs a lot; conversations with her were a source of pleasure and entertainment.

Mrs Gandhi

Can you tell me why you live separately from your husband?

I lived with my husband, who is 81, and with my son and daughter-in-law. Every day I have arguments with my daughter-in-law. She wants me to do all the work in the house. I think that at my age I shouldn't do everything – that she should help. I have spoken to my husband about it and asked him to help by speaking to my son, but he wouldn't do it. They all wanted me to do the work. There are other reasons too. Ever since we came from Kenya, 20 years ago, my husband has received the 'benefit' and he has kept it all for himself. He never gives me any money for shopping, or clothing or to buy anything. Even when we were in Kenya my husband did not allow me to go into the market – he made my life so it was like a prison without bars. He smokes and drinks a lot and then he started to hit me, so now I live separately from him.

Was the decision to leave home a difficult one to make?

No, it wasn't difficult for me to make the decision because I had suffered so much over the past 20 years and I didn't want to suffer any longer. Also my husband said to me, 'If you want to live separately, you can,' and that made it easier for me to leave. So, no, it wasn't a difficult decision and I have been much happier since I started to live separately. My husband did not think about, or want to think about my life. He only thought about his life. Now I am living separately there are no more problems. I am much happier here with no boss on top of me. If I want to go into the market I can go and no one will stop me.

When you were having problems with your husband did you find it difficult to get help?

Yes, I looked everywhere for somewhere to get help – I walked and walked all over town looking for somewhere to get help. Someone told me I might be able to get help at the Shree Ram Krishna Centre, but I didn't want to go there as I didn't think I would get help there. Eventually after searching and searching I found the community relations office and found someone who spoke Hindi and I was able to tell them all my problems and difficulties. They were able to help me. I first went to that office about 14 months ago and after about three months they had helped me to have this flat. They found people who could speak my language and they helped me with furniture. When I decided to live separately from my husband he gave me nothing. I left the house with no clothes, except what I was wearing and nothing else. I had four pounds and that was all.

When you were having problems with your husband did you find it difficult to get help from your sons?

My sons would not listen to my story. They would only listen to their father. They love their father more than they love their mother and so they would not listen to their own mother's problems. Also my husband loves his children more than he loves his wife. So for these reasons my sons were not able to help me. Some of my children were not very happy when I decided to live separately from my husband. They think that in Indian families that is not the kind of thing that should happen.

Do you see any of your family now?

I have nine children altogether – eight in England and one in Kenya. They are all married with families, and I have 13 grandchildren in all. Three of my children live in this town and five live in Leicester. They are near enough to be able to visit as they all have cars. My mother, who is 90, also lives nearby and I visit her once every week. Sometimes my children do come to visit me in this flat, but not very often, maybe once every two months. I welcome them, I welcome anyone who wants to visit, but I cannot force them to come. When they do come they are not very happy about it, so they do not come very regularly.

Are you sorry that they do not come more often?

No, I do not feel sorry or unhappy about it. That is because my children are all married and they have good jobs and so they are busy. Because of that I do not feel sorry that they do not visit me often. But I welcome them here. Not only my family, I welcome anyone who wants to come. But I have none of my old friends who come to visit me here at this place. I know very many people in Loughborough, people who I knew in Kenya. When I go into the market, if I meet people I know and they speak to me then I will speak to them. But if they do not speak to me then I do not speak to them. I go into the town nearly every day and I see people I know and sometimes we talk but no one comes to my home.

Do you ever feel lonely?

I do feel lonely sometimes. I feel lonely when I remember the past and when I think about my children. I have never lived as one person before – when we lived in Kenya my husband was often away for two or three months at a time on business, but I had the children then. Now I am by myself. But mostly I am much happier by myself because I don't have to do so much work and I don't have arguments, arguments all the time. I am also much happier now that I have become a Christian. I found that once I started to go to church and to pray to God that I felt very different. I find that my tension has gone now. My tensions were very high with all my problems, but God has cleared the body and made my heart a lot happier. I can see things differently now and that makes me happier.

Tell me how you came to be a Christian?

42

One day I was sitting in the community relations office, just passing the time, and I heard a man talking to a lady about his church. I listened to them and found it very interesting. When this man had finished talking to the other lady I went over to him and said, 'I would like to go to church one Sunday.' He put me in touch with the pastor of the church who was a bit surprised that I wanted to go but he arranged for someone to take me to church and bring me home every Sunday morning and evening. Now that I have become a Christian I have thrown away all the pictures and idols of the Indian gods. I have been a Christian now for about three months and I feel better. Sometimes it can be a problem for an Asian if they go to the Christian church because the rest of their community turns their backs on them. I haven't talked to any of my family about going to church. I don't know if that is also why they don't come to see me. They haven't objected about it, so I don't know whether they know or not.

Apart from church, what else do you enjoy?

One of the other things that I enjoy is going shopping. It is very difficult for me to manage to pay all the bills with the money that I have. I cannot buy any shoes or even a cheap saree because I don't have enough money. My husband never let me have any money, so it is very very strange to me to have to deal with money. I have to be very careful how I spend it, especially because of the gas bill and the electric bill. But I am enjoying shopping. I like to be able to go and choose what I want to buy and to eat. Every day I go into town and buy some food and come back and cook. I enjoy that very much. I enjoy it because I can choose for myself and because I am learning. I want to learn more. I want to learn to speak English, and maybe learn to read or write. Two people from the church have started to teach me to speak English. My husband did not think it was important for me to learn and he would not let me, but now I want to learn much. Not only to read and write but I want to learn about all sorts of things that I didn't know before.

Yes, I worry, I worry a lot about it but what can I do about it? If the time came when I was not able to walk or look after myself I wouldn't go back to my family. My husband and my son didn't look after me properly before, so they wouldn't look after me if I wasn't able to walk. I will have to spend that time in hospital or in an old people's home – that is the only way left for me. But I am not afraid. So long as I can manage I will look after myself and walk to the shops and when I am not able to do that then God will help me. Only God knows what will happen and how we are going to make arrangements. I haven't tried to think about making arrangements. I haven't tried to think about it because if you do then it makes you feel as though you have got problems; it makes you feel as though you are going to die soon. So I don't think about that at all. I know that when the time comes God will help me.

Mrs Patel

I have lived in this town for nearly 20 years – we came here straight from East Africa. I like it here because it is a small town and everyone is local. I know many people here, some I knew in East Africa. It is a very friendly place – everyone is coming to my house and I can go to other people's houses.

When I came to England at first I could not even say 'good morning' in English. But because everyone around me was speaking English I soon picked it up. Also, I am not shy and I don't mind asking people and that helped me to learn.

When I was in East Africa I worked as an overlocker, so was able to do that same job here at the Mansfield Hosiery. I gave that up because I became ill. I was in hospital for nine weeks and after that I didn't go back to work. I'm 64 years old now – at least that's what it says on my papers, but I'm really only 60. I was married when I was 13, but the government didn't like people to get married as young as that so years were added on to my age at that time. Now it says I'm 64, but I'm really only 60.

I have a big family, I have four daughters and five sons. I also had two miscarriages and two children who died so I have had thirteen pregnancies in all. Seven of my children came to England with me – one came over to London later and one still lives in Africa. I now have 25 grandchildren and one great-grandchild. I live with my husband and my one unmarried son, but most of my family live nearby and I see them all the time. Sometimes they come here, sometimes I go to visit them. I can drive the car now – last year when I was nearly 64 I learnt to drive and I passed my test first time. I am very proud of that – there are not many Asian women of my age who have learnt to drive, so I think it was a good example. I have also learnt how to mend machines, to change plugs and do all the decorating. It is hard work, but it helps to pass the time. I like to keep busy – if you are busy it stops you from worrying, which is good. Too much worry can kill you.

I do all the cooking and all the shopping, and every day I clean the house and I wash the clothes. I have a washing machine, but still I wash by hand – the washing machine does not make the clothes clean enough. And then I do the ironing. I like to sit and watch the T V and do the ironing. It is a lot of work but I can manage. It is good to be busy, busy, busy. It is good for old people, it is nice for them. My husband doesn't do any work in the house. The men won't do housework, they say it is women's work and they won't do it. My husband watches T V and films. He used to read but now he can't see well enough. My husband and I don't do much together now. He has got very old although he is only 73, and he can only walk a little. He likes to watch the T V – he likes the News – he likes to know what is happening in the world. I'm not so interested in that – I like *Dallas* and *Dynasty*. Many old people are interested in that, many of my friends like it. If they are on at eight o'clock at night then we will miss going to the temple that night. God doesn't mind that, he likes us to enjoy ourselves. God is your heart, you know. If you're happy, he is happy too. God says help everybody, and don't say any bad words against anybody. If anyone falls over you have got to pick them up – to help others. Often ladies who haven't got a child-minder will say to me, 'Can you look after my children?' – or if any lady wants to go to the doctor and cannot speak English, she will say to me, 'Come to the doctor with me.' I help many people because that is what God says. I think programmes like *Dynasty*, where the people don't help each other and talk against each other – that is God's little joke. We need to see the good and the bad and when we see that, we can tell that it is wrong and we know that we mustn't do that.

Every day we go to the temple in the evening, and sometimes I go in the morning. We pray to God and sing songs to God. I enjoy it and I have many friends there. Most of my sons and daughters still go to the temple. One of my sons married an English girl. I don't mind that he wanted to marry an English girl – if they are happy, we are happy. They don't go to the temple now, but it doesn't worry me. If they want to go they can. If they don't want to, that's up to them. I don't worry about other people, I only worry about myself.

My daughter still goes to the temple, except when she has the children with her for it is hard for the children to be quiet. Of course she can't go when she has her monthly periods. You can't go to the temple when you are in your periods, you are unclean then. Ladies in the house can't touch anything when they are in their periods. If there are three or four ladies in the house the others will do the cooking and serve the food and the one in her periods will have to sit by herself – the others will serve her and then she will wash her own dishes after the rest are finished. Nowadays it is not so strict. My mother-in-law would not let me touch anything if I was in my periods. My daughter-in-law when she got married I cooked for her, but otherwise she touched everywhere. Everything is changed now, but we still cannot go into the temple when we are in our periods.

I believe a lot in God. I believe that with God you can do anything. If things go wrong we do it; if anything is good then

God does it. I believe that if you pray in the heart then God will help you. I was blind before I was 20. Many people said I would never see, but I prayed and God helped me. I was blind until I was nearly 40. All my children were born and I never saw them. Then they opened my eyes. I had one operation for cataracts in Kenya and then I had another one in this country on my other eye and now I can see with both eyes. I've learnt to do many things since then, but I've never learnt to read or write and I won't learn now, because if I work closely to read it makes my eyes bad. I never learnt to read when I was young. My mother didn't send me to school because the school was boys and girls together and my mother thought that that would spoil the girls so she didn't send me. It has often caused me trouble that I can't read or write, so I sent all my children to school and they all have good jobs now. School is important because people like clever people.

We don't know how long we are going to live. If I stay well and I get old that is all right, but I pray to God don't let me stay if I get ill or bad, so that I need people to look after me. I don't want people to have to look after me. But if I do get old I have my son – my son will take us. My sons are saying, 'You come and live with me,' but I am thinking we are all right to live here yet, but if it gets so I cannot cook or look after myself my son will take us. My daughter could sometimes come here to help us but we could not go to stay with our daughter. In our culture that would be a disgrace. We can stay with our sons but not our daughters. Unless you have no one else, then you can go to your daughter, but it would still be a shame to us. That is as it was for my great-grandparents and it is still the same for us. Anyway, I don't think about getting older and not being able to get out and about. I don't think it will be like that. I think I will die quickly. I don't know, but I think that God will help me so I won't be like that. If you think that you are ill, that you can't work, that you can't do this or that, then you will be ill. It is better not to think about it, but to keep going. That is why I like to have the grandchildren around me. They make me feel young. I like to have them in the house, I enjoy that and they love me a lot. I don't like it quiet. I like the children to talk and laugh and to have friends to talk with me. I am never a lonely person. I always have plenty of people around me. Even when the children are at school and my sons and daughters are at work I go to see them in the evenings. I enjoy a joke and a laugh. I don't cry much, unless it is because some people are ill or in trouble or they die. Then I cry, but not at anything else.

6
Miss Moss

Introduction

In contrast to most of the women we interviewed, Miss Moss is wealthy. Her background was one of financial security and material and environmental privilege. However, in common with many of these women, Miss Moss has had to make major readjustments to her life as retirement and old age have approached.

Miss Moss, who is in her early sixties, lives with her close friend Cecilia in a corner house in an established residential area. Both are single, retired professional women who have been friends over many years. Some years earlier Cecilia sold her own home and bought a half share in Miss Moss's house. This means that both women have reduced their outgoings and have more money to spend on other things. Joint ownership of the house has been followed by joint ownership of one car. This combining of possessions seems to have been matched by an interdependence in other parts of their lives – in activities, family relationships, support and friendship.

The common ownership that these two women have adopted has been part of their adjustment to their reduced income during retirement. It is clear that readjustment has been just as problematic for Miss Moss as for someone on a much lower income. Restricted activity is as much a reality of the retirement for Miss Moss as it is for a poorer woman.

In our conversations with Miss Moss her responses related

specifically to her own experiences, activities and feelings. She talks very much as a single person and this is undoubtedly how she sees herself. Yet her relationship with Cecilia has been critical, particularly since Miss Moss does not enjoy good health. Cecilia is very much the domesticated one, the one who provides practical support. From her discussion of the future it is apparent that Miss Moss sees this as continuing to include Cecilia. Indeed, the fear that something might happen to her friend, that Cecilia might die first, is a very real one. By choosing to share a home these two women have found a solution to some of the problems of retirement; they have greater income, support and companionship. But the very nature of their interdependence means that they live with the worry of losing each other and all the uncertainty and change that that would bring. In this they are similar to older married women who live with the knowledge that their husbands are most likely to die before them.

Miss Moss's response must be seen within a framework that has a history of expectations, preferences and pleasures. This clearly demonstrates the theme, seen more widely in all the interviews, that the expectations, pleasures and disappointments of later life are closely connected with earlier experiences and patterns of living. Everyday life is constructed against this biography, against a context of expectations that are themselves shaped by previous experience.

As with many of her other interests, Miss Moss approached this interview with a lot of thought. She had prepared much of what she wanted to say. She chose to start with a description of herself.

I would say that I'm an independent, highly disciplined creature; I am something of a political animal, too; I would probably be labelled, quite correctly, a reactionary. I cannot suffer fools, even ungladly. I'm highly selective with the company I keep, I'm not a loner *per se*, but I do need intellectual refreshment and further search for satisfaction rather than simply socialising and collecting money.

I've lived all my life in a magnificent mansion, absolutely covered with beautiful things that I took entirely for granted as being the norm. A man who I knew led me to read Durhrer, and he said what you know is natural. This has proved to be the case. It hurt me a lot to leave this lovely home, two acres of magnificent grounds, to live in a tiny corner house in a suburban town, but I decided that it would be good for me to integrate more into society, but I haven't really pulled it off, not totally. And I don't like to mix society around very much. I'm not awfully good with people that I haven't much in common with. Of course you must have identified from this that I'm something of a snob. I would like to feel that I was more accepted by professional people.

I think my background, public boarding-school and all that, is fine, but society has changed in the last 30 years – a social revolution. I know that on the political spectrum I've been pushed further to the right than I would perhaps have wanted to have gone.

My background was, by today's standards, a wealthy one indeed. My father, whom I much admired, was a business man and who gave me an interest in money matters so that I think I can claim not only to have a reasonable interest in, but also knowledge of, such things. I am perhaps too concerned about money matters, too aware of the effects of inflation, both in the past and as far as I can see throughout my lifetime, but I am frightened by the possibility of declining standards, now that I have reached retirement.

Perhaps it would be appropriate here to give you a little bit of my sort of philosophy on retirement and wealth. In retirement one of course has more time. As things have gone for me I've had *very* much less money. Inflation has hit *independent* – and I stress independent – retired people more than any group. I ought to say that I have had a health problem and was advised at the early age of 55 to give up an interesting and financially very rewarding job.

For me, hard work and paying my way has not brought financial rewards with early retirement. Thank goodness I've always had an interest and knowledge of money matters, thus I know how to make a little less money, or rather much less money, work hard for me.

Some 12 years ago my close friend took the decision of selling her home and buying, outright, half of mine. So long as we share our home obviously we are, even by today's standards, well off, but if she were to die ahead of me this would make life much more difficult for me in the maintenance of standards which I believe are essential. Already we've sold our individual cars, we now have one joint one, that's the first major cut-back because I've enjoyed the ownership of a car throughout the whole of my life. A car to me is – well, basically it's a necessity, full stop. So, I am concerned about a reduction in my income; I am so disciplined on money matters that I consider insurance a vital part; however, my insurance premiums on my possessions and my membership of B U P A, for instance, all these things are going up and will I think inevitably be a burden to me.

Perhaps at this point I can tell you a little of what I do with the time that I have, now I have retired.

My interests are in the home – in fine things. My only interests, apart from fine things generally, concern three things and I've done some studies in depth on all three, great depth. One is hallmarking. I did for a while serve as a commissioner in hallmarking because I felt it worth doing a study in depth on the whole subject. And I have faithfully insured the practical – superb, in my judgement – collection of gold and silver that I have acquired over the years. I'm also vastly interested in Victorian paintings and reasonably knowledgeable about them. Again, it's been a do-it-myself exercise that has taken me into pastures new, and I've learnt a great deal from those studies in England. The other interest I have is in oriental rugs and carpets. Again, I've done a tremendous amount of research in this fascinating subject and I've managed to acquire a number of these in my home.

Mainly for reasons of health and wanting to discipline my life further, I decided to study for an Open University degree and here I was incredibly lucky in meeting a tutor who had opposite views to my own, but whose views nevertheless made me think harder and more deeply, and was at that particular time exceedingly helpful. Early success encouraged me to carry on and this I've been doing. If I am successful this year, I need only one further half credit and have actually wondered whether it mightn't be a good idea to contemplate a further degree, a B A Hons. in Fine Arts – History of Art in the future.

I have a passion for European culture and since I first visited France pre-war there has been a magnet working on me from that direction. This has extended, to I think about 22 European countries. All, I might say, totally unaided, in other words, doing my own thing, working from the back of an A A book and fulfilling an over-ambitious itinerary which has resulted at the end of the holiday in near exhaustion but maximum enjoyment. I'm not boasting when I say that I know, say, the country of Switzerland much better, very, very much better, than the general layout of this town. Needless to say, the pleasures of discovering Europe have been shared always with my friend. At one time my role was to drive, she looked after domestic matters, hotel rooms, very late at night, and so on, but in more recent years we've tended to share the driving – age of course does have its limitations, and one can't drive quite so far and cover quite such mileages. However, I think, God willing, I shall always be able to afford to go to Europe. After all, one doesn't have to stay always at the hotels one used in the past. In any event they are fast disappearing, alas. I think when the day comes that I can't afford to go to Europe I shall be either ashes or something else. No, I think I can always see that, it's a big part of my life.

Up till now I've talked very selfishly about myself and my interests. I've said little about my duties to society which I obviously feel – not as much as I would like to feel though. My background is one of almost total dedication to society, and even now my life continues along these lines. I'm a governor of two schools here in town, one an intermediate comprehensive, and the second an infants' school. I also consider that I have repaid some of my debt to society through the interest that I take in matters political and I think it's a pity that we English are, *en masse*, such unpolitical creatures and have no real grasp of the subject, as do the French, etc. I am a determined Conservative, a member of the local association and, inevitably, the treasurer, as you might expect, although I loathe asking anybody for anything, invariably I funk on this matter.

I was thinking, the only other things we haven't really talked about is the more practical details of how I organise my life. First I should say that I hate routine. I loathe and detest it. All my working life I've been either on a very, very close diary of interviews, school and the office visits, etc. I always had a timetable and worked to time, I loathe being timed and now that I am retired obviously I don't get up unless I have to, well, what I mean is I'm a late getter-up, so I'm not organised in that sense. But I'm intensely organised from the point of view of my possessions, everything must all be categorised and organised, but mealtimes are totally fluid and, as I say, I've loathed the discipline all my working life, having to work strictly to time. Although even now I have a fairly full diary. Let's look what I have in at present: I have a visitation to make at the primary school, I have one Open University tutorial, two visits from yourself, hair appointments and so on, one or two people to tea, a number of friends calling. Perhaps not full enough. I have been unwell, so that I haven't had the amount of planned visitors to the house that would normally have been the case, but we had visitors even so during that time and we had some planned people. Before the month is out I shall have had nearly a week with my niece in Hampshire and we are going to have one or two days down there exploring the area – so that's pretty full isn't it – well it's *fairly* full, it's full enough, I think.

You see, when there's an awful lot on and I'm enjoying myself I don't do any Open University work and, being a rather undisciplined person in this sense, then I have to work immensely hard to do three weeks' work in about four days. So, whereas I'm very organised in one sense, I'm a little bit *ad hoc* in my attitude towards my life planning. I should be very miserable if I hadn't got things in my diary but I don't want to be rushing hither and thither; I have in the past had many contacts through my interests in silver, painting and oriental rugs. However, they are not rewarding enough now because they are only fun while one has sufficient money to play with. Once that is removed then that is not sufficient, certainly not. The active side of that is over unless I were to take up a History of Art course. One reaches a saturation point in terms of how many one can accommodate in a home – I've already started to refine my silver collection and have sold off the less good items and less necessary ones. I get great joy from usage, although since I have had a robbery I've had to take measures – and obviously it would be foolish to say what they are – but very extensive measures to safeguard my valuables. It happened one lunch hour, whilst I was out trying to be helpful and console somebody who had lost a friend. When I returned I found that a robber had broken a window and got in that way. He'd gone through my drawers and managed to put quite a vast amount of value in two pockets. So I've had to take measures; I had to have a strong-room built.

It has, inevitably, I think, tarnished my interest in silverware because so many of the things that we were using on a daily basis, and having tremendous pleasure from, are now so secure that it's hardly worth the bother of getting them out, although they still come out on high days and holidays. It definitely made me very antisocial at the time because I'd worked *hard*, very hard, to collect those things. A darling clock that he took which I acquired many years ago, and with great trouble and very hard work I restored it myself, making it very valuable. So of course I was bothered, I felt soiled as all people do when a robber enters their home.

As a sister of two brothers, did you feel as a woman there was anything that you missed in terms of opportunities that your brothers had that you didn't have?

Oh, inevitably. That was the reason that I wanted to do the O U course later on. When my turn came for college my father, having retired early on grounds of ill health, was going through a rough time, and it was felt expedient to terminate my schooling – the expenditure was high in those days and of course is today more so.

My father signed an accountantship with a jolly good technical college in Leicester. 'Let her go there,' he said. 'I understand it's a two-year R S A course and it's something she can follow up from that.' I didn't want to do it and I felt then and I still feel today that I was certainly sacrificed. In the middle of this course my mother came across an advertisement in a local paper for someone to take over secretarial duties for a convalescent home. By this time the war had started, and I went along with her and took this job. We had, I think, 30 beds. These two homes were some eight or nine miles apart and in the last approximately three years of the war I ran both of them. We had, of course, trained nurses as matrons who were responsible for the nursing and I had very little contact with the patients *per se.*

After the war ended I stayed on for a year working directly for the headquarters of the Leicestershire branch of the British Red Cross Society and then I decided I must try and carve out a career for myself. It was then that I joined what was then known as the Youth Employment Service. I was paid from the word go on the same basis – on the same rate, I beg your pardon – as a man. I reckon as a woman I had to work hard and appear to be at least twice as efficient. I was a very successful youth employment officer, and when the post subsequently came up for the county youth employment service I was regarded by my own chairman as the ideal candidate. He was nearly as disappointed as I was when he failed to have an open advertisement. The job was advertised purely for men only so I had no opportunity to take the job which was rightfully mine.

In the meantime my father died and then I decided I had to make the break from it. At that time liberal studies in technical education was a new venture – the principal of the technical college obviously had been told I was somebody he couldn't afford to miss. I worked there for a very fascinating nearly two years building up this new department and was heading for quite an interesting new career. I subsequently moved to be nearer to my mother, when a similar job was advertised. So I would sum up my career by saying that throughout my whole life I've been paid as a man would have been paid, but I worked harder – yes, very much harder. So to go back to the original question of whether I felt I had missed opportunities which my brothers had: I think I have demonstrated that I didn't have the same opportunities, but I must also say that I have not been affected by this.

I think it's up to each individual to make the most of his or her life. I certainly wasn't around burning brassières, I still am sufficiently reactionary to think that a woman's place is after all best in the home, but if she has gifts and talents then they should be used and if it's possible for her to use these and do her duties faithfully in the home this is the ideal solution. I think this is very much a matter for the individual and nobody else's business really. I can't say any more than that. That's it, I've no strong feelings.

7
Maggie and Freda

Introduction

Physical disability has dogged Maggie most of her adult life. Much of her married life she has been in and out of hospital, finally losing a leg. As a result of her ill-health, she was financially dependent upon her husband, Bill, until she received her pension. Even when she was ill, both she and her husband assumed that she was fully responsible for organising the home and their domestic life. She feels that she had very little control over what she could do, or the opportunities she could make or take for herself.

Many of the things that most other women are able to take for granted are a struggle for Maggie. She has to walk with two sticks, for example, so that carrying things is difficult. Hanging out washing, getting up to put on the lights and getting ready to go out, all become major activities. Despite massive disappointments she remains cheerful, determined and without self-pity.

It would be easy to see Maggie as exploited and subordinate within a traditional marriage, and in many ways that is the case. Given that she herself recognises this, and feels that it cannot change, what is impressive is the way in which she has tried to carve out a life that provides interest, companionship and pleasure. Another view of her life would be to see it as a constant challenge to all those attitudes and forces that write off the elderly, all the more so if they are disabled. Far from allowing age to narrow her life, reaching 60 was for her a starting point. Some financial independence came with her pension and mobility allowance, and the activities organised for those over 60 enable her to visit places and have holidays that were previously not possible. She refuses to be intimidated by younger people or to stay in at night, and does all she can to retain her self-confidence. No single action on Maggie's part is very substantial, nor does she show any aggression or anger in her stance; none the less she tries to control her own life as far as possible.

Maggie's greatest sadness and anxiety is that she has no children. She believes that, in the end, relations can be relied upon to take care of you, but she and her husband have none. This means she constantly faces a future with no idea of who will help her. Her distress at the lack of kin contrasts with her friend Freda whose views are also recorded here. Maggie and Freda have been friends for 45 years. Freda and her husband had lived in one of the block of four houses next door to Maggie and Bill. Sixteen years ago they had gone to a new house at the other end of the village when the old houses had been pulled down and new flats built on the land.

Freda has children but feels they are a danger to her independence. Already she only goes out when they take her, but her main fears concern her traditional areas of control in the house. Her family now take decisions for her and indicate that her competence is in doubt. She is defined in terms of the stereotypes of her age, but says nothing because she knows that any complaint will be seen as her being difficult. Such collusion is the price of a peaceful life.

Somebody from inside shouted, 'Come on in – the door's open.' I pushed the door that opened into a corridor, and followed the light and noise coming from the room on the left. Inside the room Maggie was sitting on the settee. She picked up her stick and from six feet away deftly prodded the off switch on the television. She laughed – 'I work the lights that way, too,' – and suddenly I realised that she couldn't get up. Although we'd spoken on the telephone (having been introduced to each other by a mutual friend), this was my first visit to Maggie. She lives with her husband in an old house near one of the pubs in the village. They have lived in the house since they married in 1942. Maggie had come to the village in 1938 and met Bill there. She'd asked me to call in the evening because Bill always went to the pub for a couple of hours, and we thought we'd have a chance to talk together. Bill is in his seventies, small, wiry, but slightly lopsided as a result of a stroke two years ago. That night he never got around to going to the pub, and when he wasn't in the room with us, he hovered in the kitchen. After that first visit, though, he didn't usually bother to stay in when I called and so we had a chance to talk, just the two of us.

I was a nanny with a family here – as those children began to grow up I moved to another job, nearly the same kind of work. Then the war started and because I wasn't in an essential job I had to go into the factory and on the ammunitions. I went to Swinnerton in Staffordshire until I got married; that was in 1942, and that got me out of Swinnerton. When I married I worked for a year in a grocer's shop and then I had my bad leg, and that was the end of it. I've been ill and at home ever since. I'd always been with children, and I planned to have four – but there's no children, and so, well, that's it.

His mother and sister lived here, in this house, and we came to live with them, we were in the rooms over the corridor. Eventually his grandad died; the house belonged to him, and we started to buy it. His mother and sister moved. There was no friction, just an atmosphere. Never a row, but just a dead silence. We never had a right word; to put it bluntly, it was the jealousy of his sister. The old lady was always all right to me when the other one wasn't about. Bill's sister lives next door now, and there's still this cold war business, although she's just now trying to be more sociable. I believe she was jealous, but also I was only a poor miner's daughter – and looked down on, I think.

All my life's been affected by my leg and what happened when I was younger, and how I think and feel now, it all goes back to that. I lost my leg 20 years ago but before that I was in trouble all the while. In and out of hospital all the while, surgery, bed-rest. When I was all right, to make a few shillings I did bits of sewing for people, and we also let the rooms. When you were ill then, it was terrible. I got some panel money, about eight shillings a week but you had to pay for your own ambulance, and if you couldn't pay straight away they sent you a bill. It was 10 shillings each time. If you had to go to hospital three times a week that was thirty bob. One time I had to go every day. If it hadn't been for my dad giving us money – he even used to bring coal to put on the fire – we'd never have managed. 25 years of all this we had.

When I was 50, and finished the change, the doctor said, 'Well, we'll take your leg off to give you a bit of pleasure in your life'. [She paused for a very long time.] I don't know what to say about whether I was glad to have my leg off. At the hospital they said I couldn't have any pleasure with that horror, and so what about having it cut off. I never answered, and then I know someone put a cup of tea in my hand and the doctor said, 'Shall I put you on the waiting list?' That was on the Friday. The letter came on the Monday morning saying that the ambulance would be here at ten o'clock. So that was it. But you see, you don't know what to think till afterwards, and my leg has never really gone to me, because the feeling's there. All those phantom pains they call them, they've never gone. Some people get them and some don't. In some ways life is better now, but in other ways no.

They gave me a false leg – but I don't know, you've got to put that bloody thing on, perhaps you're going to do something and you get it on, and then you think you've got to go to the lavatory, so you have to take it off. Then while you're upstairs you stop there till you want to go again. Sometimes I get on the bed and wait for an hour. It is a trial, but I can cope with it now, but what the result will be in a few years time when I'm older and my memory is going I don't know. I'm more awkward than most because I've got two sticks, but at least I can get out – mind you, I take up all the pavement and some folks are slow to step aside; those shopping trolleys and people's shoulder bags are lethal for me. I can't get in a car easily, either. If it's a man driver, I have to say to him to look up in the air over there while I hitch everything up and get in.

It's no good worrying about the future. But you've still got to try for it and make things easier. See here, there's many a time I don't want to trade at the nearest butchers – they're expensive and aren't so good. I often say I won't go there any more, but I've still got to keep to them because they'll deliver in the winter when we can't get out. Same with the grocer. I know he's dear, but I still have to go because I depend on him as I can't carry anything. I still have to be careful even with the artificial limb – pressure points and things, and some things are uncomfy. A bus seat's more comfortable than a church seat – that's why I'd rather go on a bus ride than go to church. It's a bit of a mixed blessing really, the pain is still there. You have to do the best you can, and I'm better off than many.

It's really because of all my past that I said to you that my life didn't change that much when I became a pensioner. Life went on the same. Mind you – you went without before because you didn't know if you could afford to do things, but now it doesn't matter so much because you know the pension's there. I'm much better off as a pensioner than I was, because he never gave me much before, and now I draw it all – Bill's got the small pension from the factory. I suppose things did change a bit for me because I found I could do more. The day after my sixtieth birthday I went and asked if I could join the Over 60s club and I'm out a lot now. Last week we were on a week's holiday in Torquay with them, and next week it's Bridgmere Gardens and then Yorkshire. I didn't do these things before I was 60, but they're all things I can do easy now. You didn't have the chance before. The outings are only in the summer, but I also go to Bright Hour and Mothers Union. Monday's the only day I'm in. I go out as much as I can, particularly as I only get the extra mobility allowance until I'm 75. I've got no financial worries now, so I can and do waste it.

I've always seen to the money and bills – he's never seen to a thing. I get all the married couples' pension, but it's a bit different because I do get more for the mobility and I get another £6 now because I'm a chronic invalid. I go and get the pension from the Post Office. Sometimes I leave it there for a few weeks, or perhaps I'll draw it out and put it in my ordinary account. Then when I'm going to pay the gas and electric or rates, I'll fetch it back. I don't give Bill anything from the pension because he's got his from the factory. I pay every week, everything, and then the food comes out of what I've got left. I've just got a club now. This is the first time I've ever gone in a club, and that's via the milkman, 50p a week towards the Christmas parcel he'll bring and that will save me ordering it. First time I've ever done it. I've always looked after the money and managed, even though I told you I didn't get much. I've always managed – I've had to with my extra bits that I've religiously kept. I've only put away pennies and halfpennies.

How has your life been affected by Bill's retirement?

It didn't make any difference to me – because he's always lived his own life and still does. You see he won't go to Nottingham because he says it makes him tired. We've been once this year. He's only interested in the village and village pubs and his village friends. I don't see any more of him now than before. By the time he's been to the pub in the evening, then he goes to bed, and in the day he's in bed every afternoon because he goes to the pub at lunch time. He's always had his own friends; women as well. I'm not saying its anything . . . you know, but they flatter him and he likes that.

Right from the beginning we've never shared the jobs, even though I was ill. Mind – I think we did think then that it was our place to do it. But the fact that he never shifted anything from here to here didn't help – it doesn't occur to him; but I try and make him sometimes. If I go out, I have to leave dinner ready before I go, or like today he'll get his dinner in the pub. I don't really know how things got done when I was so ill. His mother and sister were here at first; then they left and Freda down the road did us dinners very often and she cleaned and did the washing. Even up to two or three years ago Freda used to come and help clean with me. I think I just managed. I can honestly say that many a time I was doing the jobs when the doctor came in, and I shouldn't have been doing anything. But I was and that was it, and I'm still here. I know I should have done something about it. But when I should have done it I wasn't able to and then when I was able to do it, I never did it.

You know, I did realise my situation years ago, but you see if I'd have left him, what was the chance of getting a roof over my head, no income and disabled? There was none. And there didn't seem anything I could do in between staying as I was, and the very drastic action of going. I don't think there was. That's why I can say we've never had a row – we haven't but that's because I've always just let him have his way. I've been too easy – but because I've had no chance of being otherwise. I know my sister wrote to the doctor to find out how things were, and she wanted me transferred to Oxford so she could look after me; but the doctor wouldn't accept the responsibility of my travelling. She would have looked after me, because she was upset about what was happening, but they said that part was nothing to do with them. I had to be here because of the hospital. She tried to help me and it couldn't be done.

He's always been unwilling to consider any changes. Ten years ago some flats were built next door – oh – for three thousand pounds and we'd have got ten easily for this place. He wouldn't consider it. The very thing – but he just told me I was bloody mad for wanting to leave here. It would have been a lot easier. Instead of cleaning this lot up – and now a lot of it's falling down as well – especially those outbuildings. If I'd known what I know now about getting the money and everything, I'd have gone. I've given up with Bill really. Anyway now since his stroke, he'd only get in the road, because his right hand's not so good. I do make it so that he's got to do things sometimes, or else he never would. It just doesn't occur to him.

Before we started going on these old-age pensioners holidays we'd only ever had the odd holiday together when we had a car, and he'll only go now because they're organised from the village. Sometimes we went in a caravan, but I always had to take someone else with me. I took other folks' kids because then he wouldn't say anything against coming. I took my nephew, and some other children. Bill didn't refuse if I'd asked somebody else. I knew he wouldn't, so that's how I got him to agree. Now we could both go anywhere together, but he won't come where I want to go. Today I've been into Nottingham. When it was nearly time to come back I went and had a cup of tea and got talking to someone so that I could put off having to come back.

How did you manage when Bill was ill, two years ago?

I was 67 – but I just managed. He was in a bed downstairs. One of his friends came with another one, and we brought the single bed down in that room. I just managed – carting the jalopy upstairs and everything. I had a home help, but I had to pay. It's top price, and they won't do the hard work. [She giggled.] One even put lotion on before she started. But when it's hard to manage, you're glad of even that. One asked me if there were any slugs or spiders in the house. And of course Freda came as well. Mind you it proved one thing – pub folks is better friends than church folk. He had no end of visitors.

But it's not a bad life now. We've got a routine, the wireless comes on at seven o'clock, but only low so next door won't hear it, and I switch on the kettle and then make a cup of tea. We've got it all organised – plugs either side of the bed, we can mash without getting out of bed, and I've got a pole so I can pull the curtains without getting out. At eight o'clock I get up – wipe my face with a drop of cold water, and put my teeth in and then I come down and clear up and tidy up and have my breakfast: All Bran and a cup of coffee. Bill usually makes that. I have it on here [the settee] and sit with my feet up. Then I go up the village and have a cup of tea or coffee and chat to one or two. It's usually about the weather or who's coming or going. Some only talk about pills and potions and grumble – usually those that have least to grumble about. We gossip and watch them putting money in the one-armed bandit, generally those who are always complaining that they're hard up! When I come back I do dinner, meat and two veg. every day. He grows the vegetables so I have to cook them. 'Haven't you done that cabbage? It's been there two days and I've got beans today,' he'll say. There's only Monday afternoons that I can stop in. Other days there are outings in the summer, or the Bright Hour, or I might go up afterwards to the tea shop. Nobody comes in much at night so I knit or read or watch tele and do nothing. Sometimes in the day the children come in and we play games, Scrabble and Othello. There are a couple of nights out this week. There's music at church and the Mother's Union. If you didn't want to do anything you wouldn't do it. I think I'll worry more when my health starts to go.

[At one of the interviews, Maggie's friend Freda was there.] I thought you'd like to meet her, it'd be interesting for you and we can all talk . . . She's been a real friend. I know lots of people – friendly acquaintances – but she's been my real friend. I've only got Freda like that. I've one other, but we're friends because we've got the same interests and both go to things – but it's different with you, Freda, isn't it? Doris and I go on the outings, and the Women's Institute and the church. Well Freda and I have been to church, but not so regular. [They both looked at each other knowingly and laughed.] Women make much better friends. We got to know each other because we lived near, and we helped each other; they used to come here for a bath. She helped us when we'd got no money, she used to come and clean when I was in the hospital – her and another – there was no such thing as home helps 40 years ago, but people came. She'd take our washing. We don't see each other much now; although up to a year ago Freda used to call on a Wednesday and help me clean. You were getting on 80 then weren't you?

Freda: I can't get about on my own I'm afraid now, because I fell down. I couldn't come in the village on my own. I'm all right in the house, but not on the streets.

[We moved on to talk about what was meant by feeling 'old' and whether they saw themselves as aging.]

Freda: It depends but I know I've really changed a lot this couple of years. The start of me feeling old was our Mary's death. That started it off. She was my twin sister. She died two years ago. I feel old now because I don't feel I can go out on my own. I could fall down. I don't feel safe. That's why I feel I'm old. There are days when I feel much better and I'm really champion, but then perhaps the next day I don't feel so good. I feel old when I don't feel well.

Maggie: She's right, there's no doubt about it, your sense of age has a lot to do with feeling well and fit or not. I'll tell you what I think makes me decide whether people are old or not. This morning I was in the tea shop with two other ladies. One kept telling me the same thing over and over again, and the other one was moaning. I think they're old because that's what you fear you might become like. Being old for me is when your mental power begins to go. When those start to go I'd worry. It's very pathetic and sad then. Some people I know have changed completely – particularly one friend. Her only interest was the church and the Labour party, and now . . . she's just gone. The only thing is that they don't know it. The doctor once told me not to worry over such people because they didn't suffer, but it's very sad and I wouldn't want to be like that. Your mental powers are more important than physical ailments because a lot of those can be overcome, or at least helped.

I doubt really whether you can do anything to keep your

mental powers, but you can try and keep making your mind work, and if you go out like I do it helps keep your confidence up. It's important to keep meeting people. I know, if I don't go out for some time, say in the winter, so that I haven't crossed the road for some time (because I'm slow with my leg and sticks), I get nervous and don't want to do it. I can help myself keep my confidence by crossing the road repeatedly. I don't know if your confidence goes because you're getting older, but you've got to make your mind up more and more to do things – you can't do it easily. If I didn't go out for a couple of weeks, I'd get very depressed. I get depressed when I've nothing to think about for tomorrow. If you stop in it's all work and tiredness – whereas to go out, to go to the tea shop – to get a cup of tea brought to you, and you talk and you forget yourself and everything. I could soon get depressed, but I think depression is a natural thing for the majority of people to have. It's not really associated with old age, I don't think so, no, because what young people call boredom I think can be depression in an older person. When you hear kids saying they're bored, that to me is the same, don't you think so? I think a lot of older people are bored, because they're not so active physically, and then deterioration starts. I know when you retire from work you can look forward to doing what you like. But it's no good pleasing yourself: you can get up two hours late, but then you've still got the rest of the day to get through. If you haven't any hobbies and pastimes or grandchildren or anything, then what do you do? Now I'm out more I've not done so much knitting – in fact my knitting's not so good now. I don't like the winter when I don't get out, but then I get through more of my books. I read the beginning and the end. It's got to be a very good book to keep me going because I don't read so much. I have the books on wheels, but I like a book – because I'm not a telly addict. I just like a few comedies and the news just once.

[I asked Freda if she shared Maggie's view that as a pensioner she was better off than previously.]

Freda: We're comfortable, we can manage. We're not ones for needing a lot. We don't go far, well we don't go anywhere at all now; I don't go boozing, never have; I haven't had a cigarette since last Christmas, it's the truth. There are times when I could do with one but I say no, no. I gave up at the time I started to be poorly and falling down. What I'd really like is to move from the house to a flat, and get away from the stairs, but that's all really. We manage quite well. I suppose I try to take things as they come. I'm not afraid. I do wonder sometimes what will happen but I don't moan about it, but I know it's got to come.

Maggie: It doesn't pay, I don't think, to dwell on it. You do see some old souls in the chairs, but you could make yourself bad thinking about it.

Freda: If I was on my own, I don't know what sort of views I'd have, I'm sure. But I've got my husband, and I've got children, but of course they've got their own lives.

Maggie: But when you've once got children you've got an anchor. You know that one or the other of them's going to do for you. But we haven't got that.

Freda: Well, that's true, but sometimes it's not right. One of my girls is at the house now, cleaning. She makes me cross really. She interferes too much. She says I don't look after things well enough and it will smell. She's got a vacuum thing going now, that's why she sent me out here, out the road. I resent it. I know I've got diabetes, and as well sometimes I don't always get there in time, but it's not how she says. I can still look after my house. I'd rather they didn't interfere.

Maggie: Don't you think, Freda, that she's saying these things in case it happens? With diabetes and your waterworks getting a bit of a nuisance she's probably worried in case, and just threatening you.

Freda: Last week she came in with the sole idea of complaining. I'd cleared up, and I knew she was coming so I sprinkled some Dettol about. She came in, and she hadn't hardly got inside 'smells in here', and it smelt lovely – of Dettol.

Maggie: People interfere too much with old people. I know I did with my dad. You are inclined to tell them what to do when we shouldn't. I should have respected his wishes more. I don't like it when it's done to me.

Freda: My family thinks I can't manage. One daughter lives at the top of the street. She goes to work so I don't see so much of her, which I'm thankful for. I don't want them to.

Maggie: But look, Freda, if you needed help you know they would come.

Freda: Yes, but I don't really have a say. Frank makes all the decisions, and there are times when I do mind when Frank and the family sort of gang up against me. There seems to have been quite a lot of that going off in our household lately. You see, they want me to do what they want. They keep making changes in the house. That annoys me when they want to take over in the house. Frank and the family make all the decisions — what we do; what's to be done in the house sort of thing. I think I should be given the preference of deciding what's to be done. They think I'm not capable. But I disagree. I think while I can organise the house I should be allowed to. But I keep quiet because I think, well, it's better to keep the peace.

[We started to talk about the future and who they might rely on and turn to.]

Maggie: Nobody. I haven't got anybody. There's no family because they're all scattered. There isn't anybody, which could worry me if I'd let it. If Bill falls down, the first thing I shall do is ring the police. Quite honestly, and I'm not just saying this, I honestly haven't anyone to turn to. There have been good friends, but they've gone now. I'm not saying it mournfully, but I am quite alone.

Have you and Bill ever sat down and said, 'Look, what are we going to do when we get older or if you have another stroke or I'm ill?'

Maggie: No, never, because what *are* we going to do? You see, one's going to go first aren't they? The will is made – he did agree to that eventually. I had to press the screw on that or else there was going to be a bloody mess for someone to clear up. It was after my dad died. Everything there had been done in such good order, that Bill accepted to do it. But till then we carry on. He wouldn't talk about it and I couldn't make him. He's nothing planned. At times I worry and yet what's the good – you can't. Then, of course, that's where your religion comes in. It's more or less in God's hands because however much you prepare, the unexpected can happen. I've seen that so many times. I don't really worry about the future. I'm going out while I can get out; and, as I say, when the mobility's finished when I'm 75, that'll make a difference. I know that perhaps one day I won't be able to get out and about, and might not be able to look after myself, but you can't have those kinds of thoughts because everybody can be in that stage can't they. Children are a good ally. That's my biggest . . . there's just nobody to call on at all. My sister's the same age as me and she's got a heart condition. Her husband's a lot older and he's supposed to have had heart trouble. They've no children – just one nephew. All the rest of my sisters are away – but I wouldn't expect them to look after me because of their years. It's not fair to put on anyone else. Oh yes, if the time came I should think about an old people's home. I shouldn't mind at all, if it was like the one here where you've got your own little place and your own stove so that you can do and have what you want. And there's a luncheon club. They're ideal. I'm not opposed to putting the elderly together – but I don't want to join them until I have to.

You see just now, apart from this [pointing to her leg] and my other problems, I'm able to do what I want, and I've got now that I'm not so conscientious about what I do. I know the sheets have been on the bed above a fortnight but they're stopping there. I might do them tomorrow if it's nice, and I might not. At one time I'd have worried to death – they'd have had to have come off and been washed. No, not now. I suppose

I've just realised that it doesn't matter. You see, you did it because you were duty bound to do it; well, I don't now. I suppose really that one of those modern council old-age-pensioner bungalows across here would be nice. There's only half a dozen. We've never been on a housing list. If I'd gone on one we would have had a chance I suppose, over the years. But – no, he'd never – he wouldn't refuse now, but he wouldn't do it before. And I've not gone on the list now because for one thing I don't really want to go to some areas that are a long way from the village to the shops and things than it is from here. It's too late now, anyway.

[Quite a lot of children visit Maggie and Bill. Sometimes they would be leaving as I arrived having played cards or another game, and the sweet tin was usually out. They obviously enjoyed their company and felt at ease with them. I asked Maggie how she saw the attitudes of the young and old to each other.]

Most younger people don't really respect the elderly. Mind you, a lot of the elderly are very demanding. A lot won't ask somebody to open the door, they'll demand it. I've seen it. That's why some of the kids are against old people. I've seen old women – and one or two here – their lips tighten. Lots of old people condemn the young. They demand that the young move for them, sort of thing. I've seen it. Did I tell you what Mrs Wright said to me? She congratulated me because she saw me coming down the street towards a gang of youths. She was all ready to dial 999, she said. Then of course all the youths put their thumbs up – 'Hey up Maggie' – and they walked in single file for me to go past. I hadn't noticed it the way she had because I always say, 'Hey up Fellas,' and as a matter of fact I've had chips out of their bags before now! You see it's your attitude. 'Course, I knew quite a lot of them, but it's your attitude. The same with strangers. In town today, going from the bus station to the shops I said, 'Door, fellas, please – .' They opened the door and they smiled at me and I smiled at them. It's the same at night. I'm not afraid to go out. Even if they're using that language they'll stop, and one of them has even said sorry to me. I didn't know him, although I suppose he might have recognised me. When we went on an outing to Woburn there was a gang of these foreigners and they were all chattering. There was a little black girl with them and I just said to her, 'Hello – come here,' and smiled at her, and she pinched a flower and kissed it and gave it to me, that's because I'd smiled at her. You see, that to me – I could have wept – but it's your approach and attitude. I think it's people's attitude to the young that'll make the young get their hackles up. People say there's a lot of violence about – but where's the violence in this village really?

I don't think about how old I'll live to be – it's out of your hands. I've seen such a lot of people – young as well as old, ready to die, that can't. I think I'm very much in favour of – you know what it's called when they put you to sleep, when you're really a cabbage. But, I haven't got to think about that because it's depressing. Nobody knows. I've never talked to the doctor about it – perhaps he would go into it at some time . . .

None of us know. We all want an easy comfortable life don't we, but a good many don't get it. No, you can't plan. I've stopped planning because there's nothing to plan for, only next year's holiday. Anyway you can never be sure. The only thing I can remember saying when I got married was that I wanted four children, and then what happened? You don't want one the first year do you? Anyway we were living with his mother, and then, I've never got over that disappointment. No, I'm still jealous of other folk's kids. I feel as though I've been penalised. I've had to take other folk's kids to church and on holiday. I've had none. I'd always been with children until I got married. It's the only disappointment in my life. I was never fit enough to adopt and then I was too old. It was a real gap then – but it is there now too because now I'm older there's nobody.

8
Miss Stewart

Introduction

Miss Stewart was born in 1903. Now 81, she lives alone in a terraced house near the river, in an area that has recently been redeveloped. Her house is in one of just a very few streets where the property was modernised rather than demolished. She has a new bathroom, new windows, and the house has recently been rewired and decorated. In the past many of her relatives lived nearby, but now she is the only member of her family in the area, and she can count on one hand the people she still recognises. Because of a problem with her legs, she has not been out of the house for two years now. Both her legs are swollen and bandaged. The nurse calls two or three times a week to treat them, and she has been told to keep her legs up and not to be on her feet more than is necessary. She gets around the house with the aid of a stick, and manages a very steep flight of stairs several times a day.

Most of the women we interviewed were brought up within families where the traditional division of labour and expectations prevailed. Often it was assumed that one of the daughters would take responsibility for the care of the parents. These women generally remained unmarried, and often had to combine paid employment with domestic care. While this pattern is now changing, its effects can still be seen today in the considerable number of households made up of mothers and daughters both over sixty.

As the youngest of five girls, Miss Stewart was expected to look after her parents and to support them financially. The interview reveals the gradual recognition and assessment by her of the consequences of her position as the provider of care – her awareness that she was not able to keep up contacts with her friends, and that she could not be certain of sharing the burden of care with her married sisters, even those who lived nearby. Not that she rejected the role that she had to take. The conventions were too strong for her to feel able to do that, although privately she resented the assumption that it was her job. Thinking about her position, though, she says that she knew she had to find a way to take care of herself, to establish some independence, especially in a financial sense. This became particularly clear after the death of her parents when she was in her late forties. To this end she bought the house she and her father had lived in, something that was not easy for single working-class women to do thirty years ago, particularly when she was already fifty and in poorly paid work. As she says, even her family tried to dissuade her; they could see no need for such a step. None of them had ever owned property.

Miss Stewart has done as much as she can to retain her independence from that point on. She resists any attempts by her relatives to get her to give up her home, because she values her right to dispose of her time in the way she wants, and in any case feels that she is well able to take care of herself. Pleasing herself is an important source of pleasure and contentment that she won't give up lightly: 'If I was in someone else's house I'd have to eat when they said, I couldn't decide to leave everything and read all morning. Then I'd begin to draw in and start to fit in more and lose my interests.'

Miss Stewart is something of a paradox. She talked about the way she missed many opportunities as a result of being expected to stay with her parents. This experience, coupled with those at work, has changed the way she thinks, and given her an awareness of society's attitude to women. She now argues with the young girl up the road about the importance of education, and warns her against thinking that marriage at 18 is all that matters.

But she also believes very strongly that the results of those experiences have equipped her well for her later years and retirement. Because of her domestic role, she lost her friends much earlier than most young women do, but that meant that she had time to learn how to live alone. She never expected her family to support her; now, the help they give her with shopping and heavy jobs around the house is really appreciated and a source of pleasure.

We came away with the overwhelming impression of someone who was enjoying her old age, despite being housebound. Clearly some of this must be due to her particular personality, but equally there is an important sense in which she is now 'being herself', something that for many years had to be hidden.

I lived right in the centre of Nottingham until I was 11 and then we moved to this area. At the school I went to, my teacher and the headmaster came home and wanted my mum and dad to let me go in for the exams to sit to be a teacher. They said I was teacher material. Mum and Dad wouldn't sanction it, so of course that put the top on that. So I sat the labour exam, and left school at 13. Mrs Beech, my teacher, got me an office job with Burtons the grocery people, but I didn't like it. I didn't like office work. So I gave that up and went into the Lace Market. Well I didn't care much for that either, and I'd got a friend who was working in the dressmaking trade so I went in along with her and stopped in that all my life from being 14. I worked for one firm from when I was 26 until I finished work. I worked for the father – no sorry, the grandfather, the son and grandson until I retired. That'll be ten years this year.

How did you feel at the time about not having a try at being a teacher?

Well, I've been very upset about it in after years, but at the time it didn't bother me because we'd just had a piano and I was the one picked to take lessons for it. That's what my parents said to the school, even though the teacher said I could still have taken that on with my school work. But they didn't seem as though they wanted it so that's how it was sorted out. No, I didn't regret it then, but years after I did, you know. When I was into my twenties I used to think if I'd gone to be a school-teacher I should have been on a good pension. It's not only the money, because I liked school, but I suppose – well, perhaps money has something to do with it. Mind you, probably I shouldn't have got through for as long as I have if I'd been a teacher because I would have had a lot of worries I suppose. I don't think a girl can have too much education, any more than a boy. Mind you, I think girls should go in more for the sciences and that than what they do. I think it's a good thing because that's the thing of the future for both boys and girls. I don't know whether I'm right or wrong but that's how I feel.

Why is it, do you think, that fewer girls than boys stay on at school, and fewer girls go to college?

Well I think that as soon as they get tangled up with a boy, that's the end of that, schooling goes by the board and they're too wrapped up in them. I keep telling that to the girl up the road that comes in. There's some that can keep their feet on the ground sort of thing, but the others seem to give up everything until they realise when it's too late what they've done. Also I agree that some families don't necessarily encourage girls because they have the same idea that girls are going to get married and therefore what's the point . . . me, I don't think education is ever lost. I think that today you want more education than what you did when I was a youngster because you could go out and get a job then, as they didn't ask for qualifications or anything in those days. If you were just recommended for a job people took you on and that was it.

You went on working until you were 71?

Well yes, but I'd got this house. I was on my own. I've never been married, because I looked after my mother and dad. Mother died in 1941 and my dad died in 1952. After that I bought this house, so of course that's one of the main things that kept me working, you know, because – well, I just think you've got to have money and the pension wasn't really enough to retire on then. I paid stamps up until I was 65 and so I got some extra on my pension. But they started to take a lot in tax, and so I thought to myself, well that's that, I'll struggle through some way and manage because, well, I just got fed up with paying tax and working hard and getting up and going out in all sorts of weather.

What hours did you work when you were 70?

Nine o'clock till half past four, four days a week. It was a long day. I used to be out all day. He was very lenient in that I used to get there between nine and half-past. I did that Monday, Tuesday and Wednesday. I'd have Thursday off and go on Friday because you didn't get paid until Friday. But I made up my mind to leave all at once; it was about December time and I'd had a bad time with bronchitis and arthritis and I'd been off for eight to ten weeks and I just made my mind up all at once. I thought that's it. I'm not going back any more so I went to tell him that I wasn't coming back. I was finishing. He was most annoyed about it and I'd worked for them since I was 26. All he said was, 'Oh well, cheerio, if you can't manage just let me know and I'll see what I can do,' and that was it. I finished that day. I'd made up my mind. I was surprised he treated me like that. Yes I was, really. Yes, because he hadn't done it to anybody else. As I walked down the steps I thought to myself, well, no, not if I beg my bread I shouldn't come back and ask you for anything. He wrote to me two or three times after; could I help him out, would I work for him at home? I thought to myself, no. I thought, well, what a way to treat anyone, he didn't even say thank you for all those years' service. I've never told anybody about this – you're the first one that knows about it.

Were you the only one in your family that didn't marry?

Yes. I lived with my mum and dad and looked after them. We all lived in Waterway Street and my mother died there. She died in the June 1941. There was an air raid in the May and she said it was that that had upset her. My aunt lived just above this house, and when it came empty she came up to see if we were interested, and of course we said yes, and Dad and I came down here to live.

Did you ever feel that because you were unmarried you were expected to look after your father? Did you see it that way?

Yes, I did, but I never said anything to anybody because the others had all married and got their lives, and it didn't matter about me. I was expected to do it. I was the youngest, and at home, and I was expected to do it.

And you did it?

Yes, naturally, it was my way to do it; mind you, you went against things sometimes. I was a bit disgruntled at times, because particularly when my father was on his own, I couldn't make arrangements with friends to go anywhere or do anything because of my dad, leaving him. Now I can remember we once had an outing to Blackpool and we went on the Friday afternoon and we came back on the Sunday night, with the firm. Of course I'd left my dad and I said, Now I've left you plenty of supper, and asked him if he minded me going. No he didn't. I don't suppose he did really, but when I got back he hadn't had a thing. He hadn't eaten anything that I'd left him and it worried me, that did, so I never bothered any more to make any arrangements. So I mean really you couldn't keep up with friends because you never knew what was going to happen. But I'd said, now you'll be all right, you're sure you'll look after yourself, I've left you this, and I'd cooked things and left them for him but when I came back they were all there in the larder and he'd left them.

And you were how old then?

Let me see, I was getting on, I was 38 when my mother died

and my dad lived another 11 years after that. When there were all these things going off and people wanting you to go, you think I'd love to, but . . . and towards the end he didn't have good health, so you'd got to be there to keep an eye on him. My sisters didn't do much. The eldest and the one next to me were at work, and the other one (who lived just above) used to come down occasionally if Dad wasn't well, and she'd keep an eye on him while I was at work, but they never did it regularly.

Did your life change much when your father died?

No, it just went on; you see you get into a rut, and I'd got into it. Of course, when he'd died I could get out then without any bother, but by then all my friends had gone more or less. No, life didn't change, it just went on. I stayed at work and came home in the usual way. When the owners put this house up for sale that made me think and I decided to buy it. Everybody said, 'What have you bought the house for?' and I said it was because I've realised that it will be beneficial to me. No one else is going to look after me, I'll see to myself. If I have to finish work for any reason I can probably let so much off and it will earn me something to live on. That's how I looked at it. The others [of her family] said – well I'd never have thought about it that way. They weren't very keen and didn't see that I needed it, and I said, well, you've got to when you're on your own. You have to think of yourself.

Well, now I'm retired, let me see, I just get up, I don't have a set day and I don't do anything by the clock. I had over 50 years of doing that. I just do the things I feel like. I get up in the morning, have a cup of tea, potter about doing a few jobs, things you've got to do in the house. On the days the nurse comes I'm down for half past eight, but other days it's half past nine. I only have tea, not breakfast, and I go back upstairs, have a wash, make my bed and tidy around up there, and then I'll come down and perhaps do another job, dusting or put the hoover around. Then perhaps I'll have my breakfast. And I read a lot, sometimes I'm still here at midday reading if I've got anything that's interesting. Work doesn't bother me if I'm reading, and I do a bit of sewing of course sometimes. No, others wouldn't think I led a very interesting life, but it suits me, and I can do what I want when I want.

What do you read?

All sorts, anything. I've got a card telling me my books here are overdue. Since Christmas I've read two Agatha Christies, and also *Dead Man's Folly*, *Late Rapture* and *Cards on the Table*. Because I can't go out Dorothy [her niece] chooses what I read. I've got a little secret code to put in the book to let her know that I've had it before when she's looking for a book for me. I just put a little pen mark under the same numbers as my door, so they know when they see 57 that I've had it.

Do you cook yourself lunch?

Yes, I really enjoy my food, but I don't do it till teatime. I had breakfast today about half past eleven, well now I shall have my dinner about six o'clock or half past, which I did when I went to work. I've never altered that because I thought, well, I've got into a routine and that was how I kept it. I have a proper meal, not skimped. I cook meat, two veg. and sometimes I have a sweet after it. Well, you can see with me that I don't skimp myself on food, but I've put on a lot of weight because I'm not energetic now. They keep telling me I must put my feet up and not get on them too much. It's all right, but it doesn't do any good to my figure. Now on Sundays I usually have a good late breakfast, and then I just have a tea, whatever I've got, meat or whatever, but I don't cook if you know what I mean.

What do you do in the evenings?

I should be lost without my telly. Just lately I've got hooked on *Sons and Daughters*. It's in the afternoon. I don't know whether you've seen it, it's a soap opera and it's on three afternoons a week. I've got hooked on it because there's one person in it that's quite a bitch, everything she can take advantage of she does and it sort of fascinates me. I like a good mystery too, I'd far rather look at that than one or two of these silly comedians they have on at times. There's one thing I can't stand and that's sport. Sometimes you get a nicer programme in the afternoon than ever you do at night time. Now particularly I noticed the other week, the Sweeney was on, well he only met a girl in the pub and the next thing you saw they were in bed together. Well, surely that isn't life today, surely it isn't? Everybody does as they like, but surely you don't meet someone and straight away you're in bed with them? Not unless of course that's your trade. You also see a lot of violence . . . since I've seen on the T V what's happening with this policing of the miners' strike [1985] I can see that there is a lot of violence, and it will get worse if something isn't seriously done about it. It's all right saying this used to go on years ago and it's just that we didn't hear about it, you did hear about the things that happened, but they weren't like they are today. I think it's shocking the way that the police have treated some of these men because when you come to look at it those men are fighting for a job. When you come to look at it you've got nearly four million people unemployed, there's nothing they can do, they can't go somewhere else because once they close a pit they close it; they are not opening another one. I heard someone speaking on the wireless a few weeks ago. He said it's no good many of these miners thinking that they are going to get moved to this new pit in the Vale of Belvoir because that's been scheduled for the Leicester pits when they close, so he says there'll be no work for some Nottingham miners, so it just makes you wonder. Mind you, I'm a big believer in unions.

Did you belong to a union when you worked?

No, because there wasn't one for our work. We did start to talk about it, we could have gone in the amalgamated tailors/tailoresses and textile workers but our boss said once the unions stepped in there he would shut the place down. Of course, women don't seem to want the same thing as what men do for unions, not to my idea of thinking. What I mean is they draw back. Mind you, a woman that is in the union and a member of it, she's usually a strong member, but most draw back.

Why do you think that is?

I don't know. I don't think that they've got that forcefulness that a man can get when he wants to press his point home if you know what I mean. Women should have, because when you hear some of the men saying, 'Well, their place is at home by the kitchen sink and looking after the children,' that to me is silly. If a woman has had children and brought them up to the sort of age when they're off her hands, well, she should be entitled to work and do what she wants. I don't think she should cut herself from everything because she's a mother and got a house and that. It's the same with this thing I hear the men say: 'Women can retire at 60, so why don't they bring the men's retiring age down to 60.' I feel like turning round sometimes and saying – when you men do two jobs and more a day well, yes, you can retire at 60 but not when you just do your eight-hour stint or 12 and are finished. The wife's got everything else to do, bring the kids up, and do all the cleaning, cooking and shopping. No, to me that's a very unfair world.

Are you suggesting that women have really failed to fight for their own rights?

Well they fought for them – but they haven't got them. Do you think they have? Even now, even though laws have been passed for this and that, they don't get it. They'll employ a woman, but she's got to take less wage than what a man would get in the same job.

But what are the reasons for this – why do you think it happens?

It's a mystery, but I wonder sometimes whether it's because they think that if they stand up for things they will just sort of get put down, they won't get anyone to back them up. People don't seem to support each other – I don't know – it makes you wonder.

[We talked some more about the miners' strike and current politics, about how much she enjoyed Robin Day's *Question Time* on a Thursday night, and how a lot of her knowledge came from listening to the radio. She started to tell me what she thought about the current government and particularly about the Prime Minister.]

Well I think she's done one of the worst jobs that anybody's ever done for this country, and in fact I think it'll be a long time before we ever have another woman prime minister because she's made it look as though, well, a woman's stupid in some respects. She'll neither take advice nor listen to what other people have to say, and the people that are most concerned with a particular thing and know about it, she doesn't take any notice of. She isn't opening opportunities for women. I suppose the thing was that the people who voted for her are the people that are getting better circumstances than they had before. I mean, she's not in with a majority of voters, she's in with a majority of seats . . . I always used to go and vote. Last time I forgot to get a postal vote in time, but I shall apply for a postal this time. I just don't know, she's got that . . . she was on the T V the other day and I thought to myself you don't go around with the shopping basket now, in the precincts, saying look what this has cost and what it's costing now, because the price of things is a darn sight higher now than it ever was when she came into power.

[Miss Stewart got up and went into the back kitchen to put the kettle on and make a cup of tea] *How do you manage with heavier jobs in the house, and with shopping?*

There's a girl lives next door but one, and she comes in. She goes to the corner shop for me on a Saturday, that's to get my bread and all my bits and bobs, and then she'll go to the paper shop for me. She's very good, and she'll do anything that I ask her; mind you, I give her a little bit for going because it's worth it to me. My niece brings a fair amount in for me, she goes to the butcher for me for my dinners, and she says she'll come and clean my windows and put me some clean net curtains up, but I don't bother her because she's got enough on her plate what with one thing and another.

If the lights go or the windows (but touch wood, as regards the windows, since I've had these new ones in I've been all right) then my niece's husband will do anything for me. But of course, I can't put too much on him these days, he's getting older, he's 60. He used to laugh at me when I used to say, 'Wait till you get turned 45 and you'll see how you'll slow down.' They'd laugh and say, 'Don't be silly, auntie,' but then one day to my surprise he said, 'I often think about what you said about slowing down after you've turned 45.' 'And have you?' and he said, 'By God I have.' You know you do slow – you find it probably takes half an hour longer to do a job. You don't notice it for a while and then all at once it hits you. Mind you, with my legs I'm slow at doing things now.

Do you think you'll be able to go out again?

Well I was hoping to. They're very pleased with this one, it's healing up very nicely they told me, but I get an awful lot of pain from it, and I couldn't see how it was doing, but they said it was okay yesterday. This other one isn't doing so well, though. I thought I was going to be able to get some stockings on and be out this year, but I don't know how long they'll be. This was my best leg when it started, and now it's my worst, but that's one of those things. Mind you, it's there and you can't do anything about it. If I could wave a fairy wand over it and get it right I would but as it is I've just got to wait and hope and pray that it will. It's no good being miserable about it. My sister Flo, she's got the same, she moans and groans but you're making yourself miserable and everybody else that's around you and I don't believe in that, not making people miserable. Life's bad enough without just setting out to make things worse for people. Even though I can't get out I'm not lonely. I've never been lonely, never felt it. I do feel sometimes I'd love to go to so-and-so, just go there and have a look round the shops. But even if anybody took me in a car I couldn't walk round to look at the shops so that's just a waste of time, if you know what I mean, even thinking about it. No, I content myself. If I get a bit fed up I start and do something, and when I feel better I stop and it doesn't get finished. It all depends on what kind of a life you've had earlier on. Now if I'd have had a lot of friends and lost them I might have felt lonely, but with me always having to be sort of on my own, with looking after Dad, it didn't bother me. Probably if I'd had a lot of friends I went about with and then they'd died off as they got older, then I might well have been lonely. There are a lot like that, suddenly have to get used to being alone. They don't manage very well sometimes.

What about the next 10 to 15 years?

Oh come off it, you don't think I'm going to live to be 100 do you? I don't think about it, I've only got one future.

But do you have any fears about growing older?

No. While I can keep my mind young it won't bother me. It's when you start letting go I think that . . . my niece says, 'Why don't you come to us, and why don't you do this?' Well, I won't go. I think that if you do that, you do give up. Her mother (my sister) did. I know she was poorly but she just took to her bed when it wasn't necessary. She could have stopped up a wee bit longer. I just don't think . . . I think it's a lot to do with people. If you can interest yourself and keep your thoughts young I don't think you grow old, not to that extent. I won't go and live with my family. I'd rather be independent and do what I can do and keep myself going in what way I can, the best way I can. I suppose there perhaps will come a time when I've got to give it up but, you see, while I'm here I can do as I like. If I want to go to bed in the afternoon and stop there till next day I can do it, but if you're in somebody else's house you couldn't do that and then you sort of begin to draw in a little bit. If you've spent years doing for others it's nice to please yourself for a while. I'm not afraid here on my own. It never bothers me. Now, these people I told you about further up above here, the other weekend he had to go away and she wouldn't stop in the house, even though she's got two daughters, one 14 and one 16. Well when they came back on the Sunday night the house had been burgled. Both meters had been done. I said to him, 'Why won't she stop in?' and he said, 'She can't.' Mind you it's a state of mind. I go to bed, I never think about anything, off goes the light and upstairs I go. I've always been like it, it's never dawned on me to think, oh, I daren't go here and I daren't go there.

Earlier you said you went on working as long as you did because you needed the money. Since leaving work have you been able to manage as well as you hoped?

Yes, but I have a bit of help with my rates, and being that I own the house now I don't have a rent as it's all paid for. I happened to get myself well stocked up with clothes, shoes and coats, so I've not had to buy, and I make all my own dresses and that so I don't have to buy anything, only underwear. If I'd got to go out and pay the price for clothes today I don't think I'd be able to manage really. Also, I told you I get a bit extra on the pension because of working so long and that makes it a little bit better. I don't have to do without anything, mind you I have to be careful. If I went mad with my electricity I shouldn't be able to pay the bill because even though I only have one fire I'm all electric with cooking and everything else and my bill was £118 this time. So, if I had my hot water system on every day (it's with an immersion heater) I shouldn't cope because that just absolutely eats it. The shower's all right because it's separate but I only put the immersion heater on to do some washing or if I want a lot of water for anything. I do watch how I spend my money. I was brought up where a penny was a penny, you only spent a penny, not three half pennies. They put a phone in for me. My niece saw to that, so I can get them if I need them.

Mind you, the state pension isn't enough because it's a pittance really. If you're getting another pension all well and good but I'm not. I'm only just getting the state pension because those sort of things were only just coming in when I left work. And again, I don't think my boss would ever have done it unless he was forced into it. It's all right if you're retiring on about £40 a week private pension as well as the state pension, that helps out. They talk about the average wage as over £140 a week. Well you take £43, what is it aside £140? Another thing, I'd rather have extra money paid to me and pay my own way instead of them paying it, the rates and that sort of thing. I'd rather have my own money and save it up, but you see there's so many people can't save these days when they have any money, they have it two days and it's all gone. We were taught that until you'd paid your way and sorted yourself out you didn't spend anything and I think that's been a good grounding for the older people these days. That's what makes us all watch what we are doing before we start to spend.

9
Mrs Hatch

Introduction

Mrs Hatch is 80 and lives in a comfortable semi-detached house on a modern estate. She moved to her present house with her husband about 11 years ago to be nearer one of her daughters, but her husband died eight years ago. The house is warm, well cared-for with a small tended garden. There are many pictures and photographs of her family around her room. Mrs Hatch is mobile and regards herself as being quite well, even though she needs regular medication and periodical hospital check-ups. She can and does walk considerable distances, and uses the buses to go to the nearest town, and to visit relatives some distance away. Lots of children and young couples live around her, although her immediate neighbours are a retired couple. The children play out in the street, often making quite a noise. Although this is company, they can be a nuisance and she says, 'I'm fearful for them because of the cars, and I'm also fearful about my windows because of the footballs.'

Mrs Hatch's life has revolved around her husband and family. She has never been out to work, and had no independent interests while her husband was alive. Most of their spare time was taken up with ballroom dancing, and they won lots of trophies together and made many friends. The last eight years, when Mrs Hatch has had to act as a single person, have been extremely difficult for her. She feels that, while she fills the time and gets by, much of the purpose and point to her life has gone. Her inner loneliness is acute. She believes, however, that these are private feelings and must remain so. She therefore tries very hard not to let her family see her when she is down, and she has now found ways of easing the pain. Equally, the mechanics of life – shopping, cooking, doing things 'properly', a set of routines – are the way through the difficult days. At other times these activities are a source of pleasure, company and satisfaction.

There were six of us at home, four girls and two boys. I didn't go out to work, they had me at home by 16 and I stayed there until I married. When I was about 15 I did in fact want to be a nurse. My aunt was one, and my father wrote to her about it. Her advice was not to, because you had to go for fever training. When I was old enough to actually go, well then I didn't want to anymore. So I just stayed at home. I helped with the housework, went shopping with mother and played tennis in the afternoons.

When mother died I took over the housekeeping. I was 23 then, and for the next three years I looked after them all. When I got married I remember one of my sisters saying, 'I don't know how we'll get round father if you're not here.' He was a bit touchy, and I'd always asked for anything the others had wanted. I enjoyed being at home. I got a lot of advantages, but then again I think you miss a lot when you don't go out to work.

When you get older you realise that . . . well, I was going to say that perhaps you do not mix as well. But I did mix, and I had a lot of friends from Sunday school. Then I met my hubby when I was 18. I was always shy at home and he used to say that it was because I'd never been out to work. I would have liked to have mixed more than I did, because when you go out to work you meet different people that aren't your friends and you have to learn to stick up for yourself. That's what my husband said I could not do. When my own daughters were young I resolved that they would go out to work and that they would be independent. So when they finished school they both got jobs.

[We moved on to talk about her current life, and how she spent her time.]

I've got my own house, so I do all my own work and that takes up a certain time. I've joined one or two clubs. I go to the Methodist Circle on a Tuesday afternoon, and to the W I once a month. My daughter goes with me to that, because of being out at night you see. I fill my time as best I can, my dear. [She paused for quite a long time, obviously thinking about her days.] I suppose I just fill in the time. I go to town, sometimes on my own and sometimes to meet friends. When you're in my position . . . it's so different now I'm on my own, and I really have to pass the time. You see when Robert was alive we did everything together. Now in the days I can make things to do, but the nights are very difficult. I find them so, anyway. I get very lonely, especially after having someone I did everything with. You miss them more than if you'd been married to a man who worked at night, or went out in the evenings. It's the nights that are the worst because they seem so long. The summer is better than the winter for that reason, because on fine nights you can go out. In the winter I don't go out much. I won't come home alone in the dark. When the curtains are drawn by four o'clock then it's a very long night.

I have a routine for the days so generally I know when I'm going to do things. I usually get up about half past seven, when I wake. Just lately I've not been waking up so early because I've been staying up much later than normal at night watching the snooker.

Mrs Hatch kept a diary for two weeks for us, simply recording what she did and anything she wanted to explain to us.

Below are some extracts from what she said was a fairly typical two weeks.

Monday, 6 August 1984
Got up at 8.15 – no post today. Had my usual breakfast, fruit-juice, All Bran, toast and tea. Spent the morning in the house, doing some housework, some washing and cooking dinner. I also made a phone call. No one called to see me. I always have a proper meal at lunch time – today it was a lamb chop, fresh kidney beans, new potatoes with butter. Grated apple and sultana for pudding and coffee.

After lunch I went into the village to the post office, the library and the chemist's. I made my tea, and then had a visitor. Later I had a bath and then I watched T V : the News, *The Krypton Factor* and *Coronation Street*. I rang a friend in Nottingham, and then went to bed about 10.40, and as usual read for about half an hour.

Thursday, 9 August 1984
Got up at 7.45. Fruit juice, All Bran, tea and toast for breakfast. No post today. In the morning I made a phone call, and then walked into the village to collect my shoes from the repairers and went to the butchers. Went home and made lunch of liver, bacon, onions, fresh peas, potatoes and tea. Fell asleep in the afternoon, rested and then watched T V serial. A friend phoned and I made a couple of calls. For tea I had brown bread lettuce sandwiches and a small egg custard. Spent the evening watching T V, *Crossroads,, Gambit*, and *Looks Familiar*. Two more phone calls and to bed at 10.30 to read. The phone is really my lifeline; I'd be lost without it. It's the only way I can keep in touch with friends now I live rather out of the way.

Sunday, 12 August 1984
Got up at 7.30. Usual breakfast, fruit juice, All Bran, tea and toast. My daughter is away this week, so at 8 o'clock I went round to her house to feed the cats. They weren't there and I was ages calling them and wondering what to do.

Eventually they came. Got home and did some chores – made the bed and prepared lunch. Phone call came from Scotland. Lunch was ham salad and new potatoes. Went to feed the cats again. Got back about 3.00 and read and watched T V. Had a sandwich for tea while I watched television. About 7.00 I went to see to the cats again. Got back about 8.30. Made a local phone call and went to bed at 10.00 but too tired to read.

I don't read a great deal in the evenings, but I do read in bed, and over some of my meals. I have a proper midday dinner and read then. I once saw in a magazine that if you are on your own you tend to hurry and so don't digest the food. It said that if you read you digested things much better so I started to read as I ate. I don't with my tea, because then there is usually something interesting on television, and I sit by the fire. Sometimes I do crossword puzzles. I get my reading books from the library. I always get my six books out every week. I'm allowed six but when I've read a couple by Tuesdays I take those back because I think that someone else could be reading them and I get two more, so I've always got six books here ready to read. I like a good romance and a good mystery. Yes I like a good mystery, I like to try and solve it before I get to the end. I don't like sloppy books or sexy books. Well, it's the same with the television; you get all this sex business on the television and even if I'm on my own sometimes, I just don't want to watch it, I switch it off. But it can be very embarrassing when you've got company. Well when my sons-in-law come I don't know whether to get up and switch it off, you don't know what to do. It is so embarrassing when they're getting into bed and naked. I mean they do things as near as possible, don't they? I think it puts ideas into youngsters' heads, you know. That's why I like my soap operas, you don't get that sort of thing do you? I mean, in *Emmerdale Farm* there are two pregnancies but you only hear that they are pregnant, you don't actually see, do you? So with my books and T V I do lots of things. I get a bit miserable sometimes, but you're bound to, but you've got to just think that you're on your own, nobody can do anything about it, no one else can, and you've got to make the best of your life, haven't you?

What about friends, do you have many around here?

Well, I have friends, yes, I have some good friends . . . but of course I've not got as many here as where I lived before, and as when my husband was alive. Our hobby was dancing and we would sometimes go out three or four times a week and you make a lot of friends when you're doing that but when you're on your own, well, you've just got to take things as they come. I don't go to the dancing, I wouldn't want to do that on my own. Well, I couldn't.

Do any of your friends come and visit you here – or do you go to see them?

Well, not so much here, because you see they are like me, they've no transport. I'm actually luckier than most because I have a friend in the next village, and when my daughter goes that way she can take me. Every other Friday I meet friends in town (dancing friends, of course), and we look round the shops and have a bit of lunch and, you know, we keep in touch. I have a friend round here that I go to Darby and Joan with on a Wednesday, and of course I know a lot of people, but not close friends, through my daughter, and so when I go in the village then there are people who recognise and speak to me.

You see, I'm not really isolated, love, but I do feel lonely sometimes. It's just an emptiness and feeling alone. I realise that although my daughter lives near me she has her life to lead and she has her own family and husband, and I can't expect her to be at my beck and call every time I want something. Sometimes I never even tell her if I don't feel well, I look after myself as much as I can . . . no, you can't expect your family to be at your beck and call all the time. If anything happened to me I should never expect to go and live with them, I know I could, but I wouldn't go. I wouldn't want to because I don't think it's fair. I don't really want to intrude too much into their lives. I wouldn't like to be a bossy mother-in-law. There's plenty of those around. It's not that I think I'd be losing anything if I lived with them, it's just that I'd rather be on my own as long as I can do for myself, and have them in the background. I don't want to intrude too much in their lives, and I just think that when the time comes for you to be alone you've got to accept it.

I don't mind being so, not as long as I am well. I tell people my age you know. We had a big party on my eightieth birthday, and people came from a long way. I'm not frightened of them knowing. Some people think that you're finished and boring, some, well I don't think they've really got time for older people, really old people, some of the young ones today, but not all of them. The majority of people, they're very, very good and kind to older people, but there are one or two who'd rather not know if they think you're old. Thinking about it, when I say I don't mind being 80 it's perhaps because I never think I'm 80. I never carry on as if I'm my age at all. You see I don't feel 80, love, only just odd times when I've been down and depressed and I have a good cry and I get over it. But you know how it is.

Do you think other people understand how lonely you are?

No, I don't think they do know how lonely I can get if I let myself. No. I always try to let it be the other side of me that they see. Anyway, I don't think you can really explain what it feels like. It's a hollow, and you wonder what everything is for. But it's not right to let others see.

But why is this something you have to keep so private?

Well, I think if you keep the bright side up and you're always bright and cheerful, I think you get on a lot better. People today don't want people who are morbid and miserable, they just don't want them, they just haven't got time for them, so anything like that – loneliness, being miserable – you've just got to keep it at home, keep it in your own four walls. I don't think you should show it outside because people don't want it. They've enough on their own slates without having to listen to your woes and things. Feeling lonely is a very natural and real feeling, but people like your company better when you're brighter. When you feel miserable you want to be inside your own four walls, and I've learnt that if you give way to it for half an hour or so, it passes and you get over it. I'm not afraid to cry and that helps. I'm talking now of being alone and lonely at night, and by myself, I never let my daughters see I'm miserable. Leastways I try never to show them.

You say you don't really mind being 80 provided you are well, but are you fearful of the future at all?

No, not if you mean dying. No, I'm not afraid of death, dear, I think there's something for us when we die. No, I'm not afraid at all. I'm hoping that one day, that not bodily, but spiritually, I shall be with my husband again, and he was a great believer in it too.

10
Kate

Introduction

Kate is 82. In 1935, she became a member of the Communist Party. Her political commitment had been growing for some time: visits to Speaker's Corner in Hyde Park on Sundays had 'seemed to wake something up in my mind, and I never looked back from that day'. At a meeting in Shoreditch town hall she and her husband joined the Party, after hearing Harry Pollet speak about the Spanish Civil War. He cried as he described the situation and showed them fragments of the toys the children had been playing with as the attacks against them came. 'That really affects you; it hurts,' she said. She has remained committed to the same goals and beliefs all her life, which have shaped her friendships, activities, actions and understandings. They have led to great happiness, fulfilment, and many opportunities. She has met people, been involved in an exciting and absorbing struggle, travelled and, more than anything else, has had a sense that she was 'somebody'. 'Not in a superior way but I knew I mattered as a person. I had something, we had worth and rights. It helps you along, you feel the strength.' Her commitment has also resulted in great unhappiness and hurt. She turned away from her family and her brothers and sisters became strangers. In turn, her own family distance themselves from her. She visits, they call, but they want her to 'behave' and not to embarrass them by raising politics. Their rejection of what she fights for hurts her to the point of tears.

The confidence gained from political certainty has equipped Kate to challenge many of the situations that other women we spoke to avoided, excused or accepted. She has a circle of younger women friends who visit her and help her and with whom she shares many convictions. These are her 'real' daughters, loved in an equal but different way to her natural one. Politics and friends bring her pleasure and keep her going, but they do not insulate her against the anxieties of isolation, loneliness, and a deep sadness that pervades her life, that she struggles to handle.

Five years ago Kate left the Communist Party. She still feels ashamed of the fact. At the time, it was rumoured that the communists were using and running C N D, an accusation she denies. Nevertheless she would not let her own affiliation be used by those trying to discredit the peace movement, and so she left. 'I now vote Labour, but if it were possible I'd vote Communist. It was and still is my life.'

September 12th 1940, that was when we came up from London to Nottingham. Thirteen of us crowded into a van, three families. We evacuated ourselves rather than be killed. We ran a café in the East End and the devastation was just awful. Some of them in the area said we were running away, but there was no point in dying. One of the women we came with, her mother lived in Nottingham, but we set off without telling her we were coming. We'd got seven children between us and when we got here we put the children in the front of the van. We knew there was no chance we'd be turned away if she saw them first. Anyway, she was marvellous and just said, 'How many?' and got beds and mattresses. We stayed a few days while we made contact with the Party. I'll never forget; Jack (my husband) was walking through a park when he saw a man on a bench reading the *Daily Worker*. That's how we found out where to go. Two members had us to stay while we arranged to rent a place from the corporation. It was enormous, a big old house but only fifty shillings a week, and we stayed there till my husband died. He went back to London once to clear everything up and bring our things back on a wagon. There was no point us going back to live there. I've been up here since then.

When Jack was alive we were very involved with all the political things. Meetings, leaflets, demonstrations, fighting to get people to see the injustices and how things could be changed, how we could all have the things we wanted if only we'd all use our power together. It was and still is my life. If I hadn't that I wouldn't have anything to live for, particularly now. This world is such a beautiful place; look at the colour of a sunset or the beauty of a rose and then look at what people are doing to it. I don't want this world destroyed. I could never give up working to stop that happening, although I'm much slower now and can't do so much. Mind, more people are caring now, more women as well . . . it's coming.

Jack took his own life in the late fifties. We'd run a business and things hadn't gone well. He was the kindest of people but not a business man. I found him. I'd only been speaking to him on the phone a few hours before. I tried to carry on with the business but there wasn't much help. My son didn't come and help. I love him and he's good to me, he comes here regularly, but he's weak, and ashamed of my beliefs. His wife wouldn't let him come, that's what I think. But after Jack died it was terrible. I cried and cried. I'd do anything, I'd have licked anyone's feet so as not to have to be alone. I was awful to be like that, wasn't I? I had my grandsons to stay, anytime. I thought it was marvellous and so did my daughter-in-law! They left them while they went on holiday but it helped me so much. The awful depression and sadness didn't go, though. I hadn't lost my mind, but I cried and cried. I was more like a zombie sort of thing. Eventually I went as a voluntary patient into the hospital. The psychiatrist was so nice I didn't want to come out but they kept telling me that I was well enough to go home. I was waiting to move from the big old house to a flat and in the end I came out quite suddenly because this flat became available, but I was here on my own.

The doctor was angry with my son and daughter because neither of them would have me out. My daughter couldn't really but the others could. They didn't want me because of my politics; it wasn't the depression or the fear that I was mentally ill, I'm sure of that. They are still ashamed of me. I'm 82 and still they are ashamed. Sometimes I feel awfully hurt, it's so much worse when your own reject what you believe in and have fought for. They tell me not to talk about politics. I said to them, 'What do you think I'm going to do; stand at the door waving the red flag?' But they are scared that I might damage the way people see them. They want to get on. But as long as people don't ask me to agree to something that's false to my beliefs then it's okay. I'm not going to ram anything down anyone's throat.

I've got a daughter abroad. I go and see her and her husband nearly every year. It's not quite the same there, but they still watch me and feel a bit on edge. My daughter and I have some fearful rows, she can be very sharp with me, but then we fall into each other's arms and we're sorry and we cry together and put it right with a love. But you see I need to have a break from being on my own. I need both of my children. Even though it's often trivialities, I'd rather listen to that than be on my own. My daughter-in-law came here yesterday. I asked her to come and bring her mother with her. Actually I feel sorry for her because her mum's gone round the bend a bit and she has to do something with her, so a trip here is quite nice for both of us. I shall go there next week and stay the night so that I can see them in the play they are doing at the theatre. No, we haven't broken off with each other, it's nice to get away, but it's so hurtful when they reject what you stand for and want you to pretend that you don't care about it. This year, however, I've made a promise to myself. I've vowed not to quarrel with them. It's hard when they speak sharply to you but I shall try.

I've lived here over 25 years. I like this flat and it's been nice round here most of the time, at least up to the last two years or so. There were three of us who were friends, all widows. One was a German lady from Leipzig – I've been where she came from, in East Germany – although she's gone now, but Mrs Bird was a good friend. She knew everything going on and was just so nice. I miss her so much. When I came back from seeing my daughter she told me that she was leaving. She's been driven out by the people in the two flats next door to her. This whole little block has deteriorated. They let the rubbish overflow, they never sweep up, and they borrow things that they don't return for ages. One lot don't seem to be there very much. We were told that one was a pimp by someone up the road but that doesn't mean he can't clean up the place. I will not talk to him. One of them in particular is the worst. He makes it bad for his class. Not long ago we managed to get a gate fixed to stop everyone coming through. It took ages, officials calling, suggesting different ideas and in the end doing the work. Now after just a few weeks it's been bent off the hinges. I'm sure I know who did it, and they'll drive me out. All the mess and rubbish gets on my nerves. We had one other spot of bother here before. Quite a lot of youngsters used to congregate just at the back. Sometimes they made remarks but they could be frightening by just being there. I spoke to them and asked them why they did it to us and that we were all widows living alone. One of them told me to 'fuck off' and I just turned on him with a roar and told him never to speak to me again like that. One or two of them hung their heads, and they all sloped off and haven't bothered us since. Mind you, when I told my son he said I should not have said anything. He . . . well, I suppose that is because he will toady to people rather than stand up for something. I will not do that. That's what I meant when I told you that my politics and the party have made me something, given me confidence to speak out and to see what others are doing to us. It's what I believe in, it's always at the forefront. Do you know, one of my family said to me, 'I'm not spoiling my life like you did for a cause.' I looked at him and said, 'What did I spoil? I never lived till I met these people, never knew what I valued till then.'

I've never really been intimidated by other people. It comes from my father a bit, he always told me to speak up. But it's also believing that something is wrong and has to be fought for. The system makes it harder for lots of people, not only women. So many people think they are superior and set themselves up with airs so that others are afraid to talk to them or ask questions. Not asking questions of those in suits or white coats then becomes part of what everyone accepts. I can give you a good example because I had to go to the hospital not long ago about possibly getting a hip replacement. I told the doctor that I really wanted it to get better because I had to be out working for CND. He looked at me as though I was nothing and asked me with a real sneer if I'd been in prison lately. I told him that I was too old to go to prison but that I wished I had the chance to do so. He told me the operation was a difficult one and that I 'could die . . . but you won't'. That was horrid. What an awful thing to say. They do it to everyone, but not to me if I can help it. When he'd gone the nurse said she was pleased I'd had a go at him, but of course they won't. If only everyone would realise that we have the power to change things like that if we do it together. Then people wouldn't have to be treated in these ways.

Just every now and then you find a doctor who's not like that and it's marvellous. About five years ago I found I could not hold my water. It's so embarrassing. I'd heard that you could have a ring fitted that held the bladder and I asked about it. As it turned out they don't use that approach today it seems, but I went into the hospital for an operation. The ward was nice, just four of us and lots of chintzy curtains. I had a foreign doctor who once saw me reading the *Guardian* when he came round. He asked me all about why I read it and then said that he had heard that I would like to know exactly what they had done to me. He spent ages, got out a pencil and paper and drew things and tried to help me understand. That's what we should all expect. As he was going, when he got to the door he just turned round and said, 'Peace.' It was marvellous.

I suppose most of my friends have been drawn from the Party or at least the labour movement. We've had such laughs in our time. I've met some marvellous people and some real stinkers. I must have visited half a dozen communist countries. The year before last I went to Rumania, and I've been to Russia five times. I go with people who think like me, I don't always know them beforehand. My happiness today comes from talking to friends, seeing them and meeting with people. I haven't got that many friends now, but they're from the Labour party and the women's group. I got involved with them by going to the Workers' Educational Association back in 1971. I made friends there. I know quite a lot of them. They come and visit me and ring up if they can't get here. They don't forget me, especially Rebecca. When I met some of these younger ones, sometimes they had heard of me or seen me at demonstrations and they would say, 'So you're Kate!' I love them. We've all got the same ideas. You never grow old if you've got a progressive outlook. It's up here [pointing to her head], not the body that matters, although I have to admit that since my hip went I've felt older, and I've felt ill for a few months now. I can't go on demonstrations any more, but there are things I can do. Rebecca took me to Greenham Common and I'm involved in the local C N D . Politics helps me meet new people and while I have that and company I'm all right. It's being alone that is so awful.

Sometimes I do get very desperate. I'm on just two small tablets to help me. I'm afraid. I try to think about the future, and I want to be here, but I get so depressed about it, the doctor called it a real melancholia and begged me not to take everyone's sufferings on my shoulders. I try to fight these feelings but sometimes I want suicide so as not to have to think. I understand now how desperate Jack must have felt, but what courage he must have had to do it. I always try to see how small my sorrows are compared to others, but often other people's are overwhelming to me too. But while I can get out and meet others and work then things are fine.

Most days I go out or someone calls. I suppose I go into town three or four times a week to the shops or the library. The bus pass is a real help, although I'm not really short of money and can manage quite well. I know a lot of them that are on the bus now. I just sit down and chat about what's going on around. Quite often someone says, 'I remember I've sat with you before. Are you all right?' and we go on from there. It's the same in town, quite often there is someone I know or that you get talking to. I usually go into town in the afternoon. I deliberately try to get into conversations with people about the cost of things, say, if I'm in the shops, and then point out to them why I think everything is going up. A lot tell me they're not interested in politics and that they don't know anything. I tell them how wrong they are, that they know such a lot and that politics is economics and how they could change so much. Sometimes they're a bit rude or nasty with me and I find myself getting cross with them, and then I feel down and sad for a while. At night there might be a meeting, but I've noticed that it's quite hard to keep groups going on estates like this and at the moment there aren't meetings. Sometimes in the summer I'll go for a ride out into the country, not so much now because of my leg. Most nights I read, or watch the television. My son comes about once a week and usually at the weekend Rebecca comes and sometimes her friends. Those are the times I like, when I'm with those that think the same way.

They gave me a marvellous surprise when I was 80. Rebecca just asked me what I was doing on Sunday and because I said that I'd nothing arranged she said I should pop down and have a cup of tea with them. Do you know, everyone was there, one had even come from London. They're so kind. It was marvellous.

11
Mrs Pullan

Introduction

Mrs Pullan had been retired from full-time work for nearly two years when we first met her. For most of her adult life she had been a teacher, particularly concerned with handicapped children. She lived in a purpose-built housing complex not far from the centre of town, where there were between 50 and 60 retired people, mainly women. Her flat was comfortable, with lots of pictures, some books, and a cat that she hadn't wished for but now indulged and wouldn't want to be without.

The housing complex was two years old and situated in an area that was being improved. The development consisted of two-storey blocks each containing eight flats. There were some communal rooms, and a well-planted garden in the middle of the complex, with benches and seats. If you arrived by car, as we did, you parked at one end of the flats and had to walk right through the development, passing the lounge and the garden area. Although we visited at several different times the place always seemed deserted. Nobody was ever in the garden, and rarely did we see anyone in the lounge. There was a fair bit of rubbish blowing about and a lot of noise from the surrounding streets where a lot of rebuilding and improvement was taking place.

Retirement has been a very difficult experience for Mrs Pullan. Her account of the past few years shows the power and impact of a society where status, self-confidence and daily organisation revolve around work. Her account is one of a search for an alternative structure and a very frank and thoughtful discussion of why it is so difficult in general, and what it has been like for her in particular. As she puts it, she not only wants the chance to develop and pursue her interests, but to have 'some peace and comfort and tranquility. You shouldn't have to keep fighting and asking and sorting out.' Retirement has enabled her to see clearly society's lack of interest in the old: the lack of adequate help to prepare for a major change, and the process of what she terms 'making gestures', 'doling out' rather than valuing and caring about the elderly. Awareness of these attitudes has come late in life, and it has all been so different to what she expected. This has only heightened her sense of rejection and anger. Many of the disappointments have crystallised around her housing arrangements. She contrasts the apparent support for the elderly in the provision of purpose-built accommodation with its reality for her: the lack of choice, the terrible noise, intimidation from those who live around, and lack of concern and response from those managing the complex, even though she has tried to draw their attention to some of the problems and anxieties faced by the residents. It is in these parts of the interviews that Mrs Pullan's anger can really be sensed. She has in fact decided to leave her flat, even though the move itself is a financial worry. When we last spoke to her she was due to leave within a week to live on her own in a rented house in the suburbs. Here she felt she would at least be more in control of her environment and away from unacceptable impositions in one area of her life.

Mrs Pullan would, however, be the first to acknowledge that she has been lucky to be able to move. She feels strongly that she has been driven out by the attitudes of those in authority. Their attitudes towards the elderly are particularly damaging, she told us, because this group is one that cannot fight back. She sees age largely in terms of declining strength and a lack of energy. Other people must fight to change things for the old. She told us that many people in the complex were hurt by how they were treated but 'because you've not got the fitness stored you haven't got the physical ability to get up and get out and do something about it'.

I don't think I mind being old, I try very hard to accept that I am old, but what makes it harder is that other people think that old age is a write-off, so it makes it very difficult. Their attitudes to old age make it very difficult for you to accept it. If only people would regard it as something that . . . you know, when I was very young I never thought I would ever, ever, grow old, it's something that's inconceivable when you're very young. Can you imagine it? I couldn't imagine it all, but you just journey through life and then suddenly you are there. The reason it's brought home to you with such a jolt is because you give up work. You have to give up work – suddenly.

You see, I've spent many, many years in a job. I was a teacher, mainly secondary children. I didn't go straight into teaching when I left school because I was brought up in an orphanage. When you left school – I was 17 – you had to do what they called a year in the house, helping. Then when I told the governor that I wanted to be a teacher he said they couldn't consider paying for that because my father was still alive, even though he couldn't afford to pay. Instead, I went to a tiny insurance office, and then during the war into a factory. When the emergency training scheme for teachers came along after the war, I thought, here's my second chance, and I got in through that.

I taught in several places, and gradually specialised in teaching children with special needs and I became the 'reading' expert. During my first job teaching I met my husband [she laughed]. Now, that was a disaster too. He lived in York and so I moved there to teach. I was divorced after three years, and it was really after that that I went into special education. After 20 years teaching I actually left for a while because I felt completely drained, both physically and mentally. I didn't plan that very well though and while I did try some other jobs, hotel work for example, in the end financial necessity made me creep back into teaching. I managed to go back to the school I'd been in and I was really very happy there. As I came up to retirement (at 60) I decided I really wanted to stay on for a couple more years and spend some time organising my retirement. In fact it didn't work out that way because there were changes at the school and we had a new head and suddenly reading didn't really matter, so I decided I had to retire, even though I wasn't really prepared for it. I was really rather bitter in my last years. I felt forced out before I was ready, because what I did was no longer a priority.

Work was very busy. I helped small groups of children all day, 20 to 30 minutes for each group twice a week. Evenings were often dull. I used to do a lot of courses. I felt morally bound while I was being paid any money that I must keep up to date so I did try. Three weeks before I retired I was on a weekend course on spelling at the university. I could have spent all my spare time doing that, and I tried to make it foremost so that I should know what was going on. But I didn't spend all my time on school work. I found housework therapeutic, and I entertained. I like cooking and I used to go to the theatre with friends, or on my own. In the last year of teaching I was thinking about retirement, but up until then I was content, with a reasonable life that was ticking over. The thing about life at work is that it has to run along these rails, so you feel safe inside the rails. When you've given up work there's no timing, no guidelines, nothing. I was absolutely bewildered. As I came up to leaving work I was bitter, cynical and very cross that I couldn't stay at work at least one more year.

Did you look forward to having more time to yourself?

Yes I did, of course I did. I thought that was lovely and I liked the idea of not having to jump when somebody said, but I think I wanted more time to adjust. I felt all of these things at the same time. I really believe that it's the most difficult thing

I have done in my life, it's like the huge change from school to work, but because you're young then you go blithely into it, completely unaware of all the adjustments you've got to make. You go into it with a lot of confidence even though the changes are tremendous. Similarly, the adjustments from working all the time to no work are equally great but they're much more daunting because you're older and haven't the youthful confidence to sail into it and think I'll do it come what may.

I did think about retirement beforehand – and I did two pre-retirement courses – one arranged by teachers, and the other at the local poly. I heard about the first one at school, but it was full. Anyway, I said to the man organising it that I knew I would need a lot of help, and I think I persuaded him that my need was greater than anyone else's. When a vacancy came they phoned me and I took it. I enjoyed it very much; four separate days and it was helpful but not enough. There wasn't enough time spent on it at all, you just glossed over things and although I took notes, there was no time to discuss ideas with someone else who was going into the same situation. It was helpful and dealt with lots of aspects, but it didn't go deep enough. One of the best things I got from the course came from the opening. I remember it very clearly, because I was just on the point of doing what the speaker warned against. It was opened by a councillor, who was in her seventies. She said, 'Keep your standards up, dress and appearance. Just because you've retired don't become sloppy.' I was exactly on the point of doing just that; I thought, lovely, I needn't bother, I can wear my slippers. I was ever so glad of that advice. I thought about my friend in Wolverhampton who has just retired. She has bad feet and she was on about creeping into her slippers. I told her she mustn't while she was at home, you must wear shoes and put your slippers on in the evening! I try to do that now.

The second retirement course I liked a lot because there were general members of the public there (the other one had been all teachers), so you got diverse opinions. You see, you worry about what you're leaving behind you, but you quickly learn you're not going to do anybody any good by worrying. I remember this one man saying that what worried him was that those continuing at his work were in no way interested in the skills that he had acquired over the years and he would dearly love to have passed on a little bit to them. I'd found exactly the same because I'd gone into reading in depth, and I'd lots of tips and knacks about how to do things that I knew would be really useful, but no one wanted to know and that hurt me. I'd thought about using computer games to help develop concentration, and I'd collected a lot of equipment to encourage and help readers. No one wanted to know about that.

As you came up to retirement, what were the things that you thought about most?

Well, first I was anxious about whether I would be going the right way about acquiring a pension, what did I have to do and how would I be paid? The cash side of retirement was a tremendous worry at first because I didn't know anything. But I needn't have been concerned because D H S S were very competent and everything was covered and I'd no cause to be anxious. But I was also worried about the lack of companionship. No, not really that, more the daily social round. There were people there at work to talk to, to grumble to; they talk to you, you've had that for years and taken it for granted and you realise suddenly it's not going to be there at all. There were going to be no people in my life, there as a matter of course. You'd no choice who they were, some you don't like and don't get on with, but they were there and interested and they did ask you questions. Suddenly there is no one. The retirement courses didn't discuss this even though I tried to get them to. I was frightened that I would be alone and severed from everything, and it still hasn't gone. I'm still afraid of loneliness and really as a result you grab at the chance of seeing people and visits; almost greedily in case there isn't another chance. I'm sure there will be, because people do phone and call and ask you to do things, but I'm still afraid and anxious about it.

Another thing that has happened since I left work is that I

feel an awful exposure of what I know are my own inadequacies and inabilities, about how to deal with lots of things – silly things, often practical, but I hate it, and I feel most uncomfortable with it. When it came to moving here I was uncertain, indecisive and didn't know how to go about things. I must lack business acumen or something, but for instance I had trouble with the furniture removers. I found some, but they were virtually non-existent when I went round to the place, and the Indian bloke standing next door said, 'I wouldn't bother with them if I were you,' and this was the day before I was moving and I hadn't a clue what to do. I got through by luck because the man doing the carpets knew somebody and he phoned them and these fellows turned up and helped me. But I was completely at sea and very distraught and upset and it was very obvious. I've been in situations that I haven't known how to deal with before but it hasn't been obvious to anyone else. I've been able to conceal them and muddle through or do things badly, or not do them, because they were only a small part of my life when I was at work and didn't stand out, not to me, nor to anybody else. But it's different now. They look very large. I got to the crying stage over these inadequacies at times, because I didn't know what to do. I haven't come to grips with that yet, it's still there. All these things I'd been able to conceal, because I hadn't needed to reveal them, they now loom very large and seem more visible.

Even when I was at work free time often got taken up with getting ready for work. Obviously I could do nothing if I wanted, but that didn't happen very often and so I did look forward to more time. And then when you suddenly have it you realise there is nothing there any more, literally nothing. It's odd, but after I'd been out of the orphanage for a while I had this great urge to feel free and not to have the discipline of a job or anything. I wanted complete freedom, but of course I couldn't have it. Well now, along comes the chance, no work, nothing, along comes complete freedom, what I've been looking for, but now it's here I don't want it. Somebody with a husband or daughter or someone, at least has a certain amount of structure there because they have to consider someone else. I don't have to take account of anybody else or their feelings or thoughts. So you see there is nothing to be said for complete freedom. I used to enjoy reading very much indeed, a great variety of stuff, including work things, but I enjoyed it so much. I can remember thinking how wonderful to be retired because I'll have so much time to read. Do you know, I have done much less reading of any kind. Every now and then I make myself go down to the library and get some books. I do read them, I make myself, but it is a tremendous effort, and it's not the kind of reading I wanted to do. I feel really, really cross about that. Another thing that's happened is the piano. Years ago at the orphanage I was a guinea-pig, in that some-one could have piano lessons and I was chosen. I don't think that the teaching was very good, and I can't play much now and my sight-reading is so slow. I decided once I was retired I would start again. Now I am retired I don't know whether I can do it. The prospect of deciding about buying a piano frightens me, and also how will I make myself sit down and play. They told me I could use the piano here, there's one in the room on the other side, but I've never ever been over. These things are odd, and peculiar and sad.

You see, even after two years of retirement I still haven't established a framework. I'm still floundering and I just envy those people who have worked out a way to live.

In a sense my retirement got off to a bad start. I had very mixed feelings, and I suppose I didn't really feel prepared to retire, but the people around me were helpful. At that time I lived in a block of flats; I rented one, and next door were some students. I'd met one of the girls at the bus stop and we'd become friends. They were all nice to me but one girl had finished her course but she couldn't get a job so she was at home all day. She needed a bit of help and support and I think I was able to be useful. I enjoyed those girls; they were very helpful indeed during those first few weeks. Then I decided to go and spend a short holiday with a friend who had retired to Bournemouth. Just before going I went to the dentist and I was grumbling about being retired. He said, 'Well if I were you I'd make up your mind you're going to enjoy it.' I went away thinking I would decide to enjoy it. I would make my mind up to enjoy it. I went sailing down to Bournemouth and came back thinking, now is the time I'm going to do all the things I've ever dreamed of doing. And then, when I got back in the autumn I found I had to look for somewhere else to live. It was awful. I suppose I spent six months, all of that time searching for accommodation, trudging about in the cold and the snow. I started a French class, I can't remember what else I started, but I became dispirited and I gave up nearly everything I'd begun. From then on I went into a decline and I really felt poorly. By Christmas I'd got an abscess in my mouth and I felt awful; I had all kinds of things over the next few months, all just stress, there was nothing really wrong at all, I was just struggling to come to terms with retirement and finding somewhere to live.

By the spring I'd found this housing, but I knew almost straight away that it wasn't right and I didn't like it. But I realised that I had to get fit and develop good health, so I joined a fitness class for over fifties and loved it. I've gone back again this year. I just was determined to try. I joined the migraine group and found the relaxation course that has been so helpful. I've tried to take more care with my diet. I started swimming but I haven't pursued it. I made a conscious decision to try and get my health right, and to see that I went to bed at a reasonable hour. I tried to get a routine and not be sloppy about things. But there's also a link with mental health, because I did get depressed. I've become friends with someone who asked me if I'd read a particular book that she said would help, *Self-help and Your Nerves*. It's so helpful and supportive. I also bought something about asserting yourself. I've found those kinds of things that I've read very helpful. 'Float through it', 'float past it', they tell you. They are self-help books, and if there is nobody else you've got to help yourself, haven't you? If you're on your own, you do need to have confidence. Now I had it before, both in my job and myself. I had the confidence, but a lot of it has gone, in part because I think feeling confident has a great deal to do with being fit, so I must keep on working at being healthy and fit.

If your ideas about retirement haven't quite worked out, can you tell me how you do spend your time?

Oh, heavens, I knew this would come and I've decided that I must just write down what I do do some days, because I never seem to have a spare minute. I've got a bowlful of washing in there that's been there since last Sunday and I literally haven't had time. I haven't done it yet. I keep thinking I'll do it tomorrow, I'll do it tomorrow. I'm so badly organised, but I would really love to be well organised. A friend of mine in Wolverhampton who's retired amazed me when by chance I asked her something and she pulled out a folder and everything was neat and tidy and organised. [She laughed] I went out and bought a whole lot of folders after that but I still haven't used any of them. I want to be more like that, I'm struggling and trying, and I have a little go each day. I came here with a great pile of unanswered correspondence, thinking I'll do it, but there are some people I still haven't written to yet.

But, how have I spent today? The alarm goes off at six thirty and I spend the first half hour now talking to the cat. I said I wouldn't have a cat, but some friends persuaded me. She's got a little box in my room, but she usually ends up with me. I listen to the radio. In fact I used to be an ardent listener, but I'm doing much less of that now. I say it's because of living here and not wanting to disturb the neighbours, but I'm not really sure that's true. It's like television, I don't look at that as much either, and I've got this lovely brand new colour T V, I've always longed for one and I've had one since I retired, but I don't look at it as much as I did the old black and white one. I usually have a bath, and play with the cat. I say to her, 'Go away, I can't spare the time to play with you.' I was very preoccupied this morning with the move I'm about to make. I keep thinking it over and over. But then I did get on and got ready to rush into town. I had to clear up before I went. After going to the bank I met a friend, oh and on the way out I met an old friend who I hadn't seen for ages. We agreed to ring each other. I will do it, even though I leave it, I shall do it. I've got a friend coming this evening so I did some shopping and then I came home and did a few bits for tonight.

I go out most days. At one time I made a point of going out for a walk every day, but I haven't been doing just lately. It suited me because I used to think whether I'd like to get a house in the areas I went through, but I realise that some days I overdid the distance. But I find it difficult to make those kinds of judgements, I overdo it. When I decide to do something, often I do it to the extreme. I find it very hard to moderate things. Not long ago I tried to get more organised by using one of those diaries that allows you to plan the week. I tried to mould a routine a week ahead, but I've stopped doing that now. People ring me, and we write and some people pop in, but it's all a bit haphazard. I go to evening classes. I've pursued that more than anything, and occasionally I go to the theatre or meet ex-colleagues in town; but much less than I used to.

I was also worried about money when I retired, but I suppose I've got by so far. I'm not a good manager, I've never been extravagant because I've never had the money to be so. Even when I worked I only had a holiday occasionally, but I was quite happy. I don't suppose I'll have any now. Since I've retired I think that I maybe don't have just quite enough money to do the things I'd like to do. When I retired I had a very nice insurance policy that matured, and I bought my television and paid off some furniture. Since then I've had another one. I haven't spent it all yet but I'm gradually dipping in to it, so I'm not managing on the pension – no I'd like to be much firmer with myself, and see if I can't manage. I couldn't live on just the state pension, not at all. Some people have to but it's a real scrape for them, and sometimes it can only be done with a very, very narrow existence. It's grossly underpaid, it's not enough, and they all have to have help from their families. I don't really worry about the money, but I know that there are things I can't pay for out of my pension, like holidays for instance. But this place has brought home to me a lot of the attitudes to the elderly.

Living here has not really been a very happy experience. It's more secure than a private rented flat – but at a cost – and I've decided that I have to move, even though I'm very anxious and uncertain about the move. It has taken me a long time to decide and I'm worried about whether I will manage the garden and silly things like will the curtains fit. It is also quite a long way from town and I don't know anyone there, so that's a concern, but I've decided to go.

I've come to the conclusion that housing complexes for retired people are wrong – that is, if they're all like this. You feel as though you're inside an institution. Several people here have literally cried while they've been talking to me, particularly in the early days last year, because they've been so unhappy. I'm not making that up. They feel that the place is not right for older people. If it is for older people we want it to be a good deal quieter. We don't want to be bothered with all the local people constantly haring through the place and staring up at you. Some people have been intimidated by the youngsters nearby poking fun at them and throwing cans. This hurts older people because they have every right to be here, yet feel ousted. I think the problem is highlighted by the fact we are all stuck together in this little community, all concentrated together. Also, if I'm really honest, I think the wardens don't really care. I haven't seen the warden for months, and when I saw her once in the hairdressers it's just, 'Hello,' as though she's someone I haven't seen for ages anyway. One lady here used to be in another complex. It was smaller but the warden came round every day – just walked round and said hello. She didn't stay long. I know this lady feels not as happy here as there. Also there are lots of things wrong with the structure of the place. The heating's most unsatisfactory. All through the hot weather the heating was on, and people lived really miserable lives. This place has been open over a year now. If I'd been the warden I'd have moved heaven and earth and gone to the authorities and said, 'These are my old ladies, will you please get something done. I will not give up.'

I decided that we had to take some action, and I decided to draft a letter to the Association listing the problems, but it hasn't brought any change and they obviously resent my pointing out how we're being treated. We've also had quite a lot of problems with security and outsiders wandering in. The solution has been that the main doors to the group of flats is locked very early. One time a friend came to visit me about eight o'clock and she couldn't get in, or make anyone hear, or find anyone to ask what was happening. In the end she went home and rang me up from there and so I didn't see her. We shouldn't be scared by others and have to live as though we were in a fortress. A lot of people here are frightened to go out as well. I'm not, but I'm unusual. I know this area well, and it's not far from the bus stop and the streets are well lit. Most older people feel vulnerable and at risk, though, and they respond by isolating themselves further.

This complex is particularly bad, but I do have reservations about them all unless they are structured differently. There should be an element of choice. All the flats here are exactly the same but there should be a little bit of choice – Do you want a big sitting-room, or a little one? They are all very uniform. We are responsible for the interior decor so that gives some variety. One lady here told me, though, that she'd absolutely no intention of doing anything at all because she was so unhappy. 'And just wait till they've finished that pub, our lives will be a misery,' she said, referring to the pub that's being built over the road. We had a great deal of noise all summer from the pub and the street. All the lounge windows face the street. The noise is abominable, the pub, disco, car doors, shouting and screaming. It would have been better if the kitchen had been nearest the street and the lounge at the back. What I feel is that they've got this pattern, these housing associations; 'This is right, just throw it up quick, let's get the old people in and settled. We've done something for the old people and made a good show of it.' But really there's no thought behind it whatsoever. The people here are now talking about wanting a great big wire fence put up to stop people coming over and playing and throwing bricks and stones, and dogs and dog muck, and destroying the saplings and shrubs. It could have been lovely. There's a garden, but no one sits out because of the abuse.

But, you see, I don't think people care about the elderly. What I've seen these last two years and experienced is so different from what I expected. Did I tell you about when I was young, about travelling on trams and buses and how we automatically stood up always for someone older than us? I used to think, 'How lovely to grow old, I'll always have a seat on a bus.' But you see how society has changed quite remarkably and it's not like that any more. I don't believe that by virtue of the fact that you're old that you are automatically entitled to this, this and this, I don't believe that, and I think you still have something that you can put into society, but there has been a change in general attitudes, and it's felt. The people here notice things and they're hurt by it. Because they're old they haven't got all the strength and physical ability to make a big fuss about things but they should not put up with some of the things they do put up with. There's a certain air of apathy here, and it's because even though people are aware of the fact that things aren't right, as you get older your physical ability declines and so it's harder to do anything. I notice it. I was trying to lift something the other day and couldn't and I cried out to my visitor, 'Oh, I could lift this last year and I can't move it now,' and he said, 'You can't store fitness, you know.' That's the worry, because you've got to keep on at it, or it goes and then you can't tackle things. But because you've not got the fitness stored you haven't got the physical ability to get up and get out and do something. Now that's just because you're old, and it shouldn't be that you have to keep fighting and asking and sorting out. Old people have put into the world and worked hard. We're entitled to some peace and comfort and tranquility which is all that's being asked. We shouldn't have to go down on bended knee. We should not be subjected to a lot of things that go on and have certainly gone on here. It's very unfair. I've told you before that other people write old age off and it's so unfair.

*You've said several times that you are entirely on your own,
without any family. Do you think about the future?*

Yes, yes, I do, but how can you have plans? I'd love to have
some plans, but how do you know. I've no real idea how I'll
look after myself – only very vague notions. I mean I've said
that I don't like this type of housing, that I'm curtailed by it
and don't want to stay here. But I realise that probably this is
where I shall be again one day if I live. You see, you begin to
think about how long you'll live. You can't really plan, but
vaguely I think that one day I'll come back to this type of
accommodation – but somewhere better organised than here.

12
Mrs Foules and Mrs Irwin

Introduction

Mrs Foules and Mrs Irwin were both born in the final decade of the last century, Mrs Foules in Loughborough, Mrs Irwin in London. At present, women of 90 still account for only a small proportion of the over-sixties, but the trends suggest that this will become a growing group. Younger women find it difficult enough to contemplate life at 60, yet the reality is that many will live to 90 and beyond. These interviews show something of what life is like at 90 and how different it is from the lives of the 'young old'.

Several of our interviews show that as we get older time perspectives change; it is often the earliest years that are recalled and given prominence rather than the mid years. Both these women experienced two world wars as adults. You might expect the Second World War to be more easily remembered, but this period appears dim in their memories compared to the clarity with which the First World War is recounted.

Both women worked in factories during World War One: Mrs Foules in textiles, making army equipment; Mrs Irwin in munitions. It was at the factory that Mrs Irwin met her husband. He had been conscripted into the munitions factory in London. After the war they returned to Loughborough as husband and wife. Mrs Foules' wartime romance did not end so happily. Her fiancé was wounded in France, returned to England for a long period of convalescence and was subsequently drafted back to France where he was killed. Some years later Mrs Foules did marry, but she had no children.

Knowing the recent past-histories and present-day situation of these two women, one cannot fail to be struck by the similarities. Both are around 90 years old, living in warden-controlled local authority accommodation; both moved to their present homes with their husbands around 17 years ago, and both were widowed within a year. Both women still care for themselves and enjoy reasonable health, although both now suffer from swollen ankles due to water retention and this is gradually decreasing their mobility. They enjoy remarkably good eyesight and hearing; Mrs Foules' memory is still very acute, but Mrs Irwin is beginning to find this something of a problem. Both attend different day centres on two days in the week, being transported there by volunteer drivers. Both women also see some members of their family regularly. Despite all these similarities, Mrs Foules seems better equipped to cope with the situation than Mrs Irwin. Individual histories and temperaments inevitably bring about different responses from each person. The interviews show that assessing the objective quality of a person's life or devising a 'solution' for old age cannot be based solely on standard criteria. To do so is to fail to see the individuals behind the 'situation'.

Mrs Foules is a small, smartly dressed, well made-up woman, who obviously enjoys talking and having a thoroughly good chat. Her appearance is important to her and she still gets great pleasure from having new clothes. Mrs Irwin, while very neat and tidy with beautiful white hair, is less interested in how she looks. She is a quieter, thoughtful lady, and while she enjoys having visitors and appreciates the companionship, her conversation is more reflective. She is a very, very lonely person — she hates her lack of mobility and the limitations and increased dependence that it has brought. She does have several callers, although they often do not stay long, and this is not sufficient to overcome her great loneliness. She thinks that one reason for this may be that she cannot gossip and doesn't enjoy talking about other people's private lives, or exchanging confidences about her life. Frailty and restricted mobility obviously reduces the range of activities possible in old age, leaving conversation as one of the few remaining options. However, as we see here, conversation and simple social exchange do not come easily to everyone.

Mrs Foules thoroughly enjoys a lively chat or, if you like, a good gossip. She had several neighbours popping in while we were visiting and they told each other all the news. She is also a good story-teller. She has a whole range of stories both about past events in her own life and present-day events in the town. She told in great detail of one night the Zeppelins dropped their bombs during the First World War, and of her attempts to improve her working conditions in the hosiery factories through the unions. Although she tells marvellous tales of the past, one never gets the impression that she dwells there, rather that she is a woman who lives for today; she takes every opportunity that arises and expresses few, if any, anxieties about life.

> Last week we went on a canal trip – the people from St Mary's arranged it. I had never done it before and I did enjoy it, the weather was lovely – well, it was a bit cold, but nice and dry. We went to the boat by car and then went down the canal in the narrowboat. We stopped at a pub on the river for lunch; it was just a cob and that, but it was okay and it was all ready for us. When we were sitting at lunch a lady said to me, 'Are you Sally Lawson?' and I said, 'I was once, but I don't know who you are.' 'I'm Edi Plait,' she said, and it was a girl I was very friendly with when we were young. I hadn't seen her for years – oh, we did have a good chat.

This lively, almost adventurous attitude to life is in marked contrast to that of Mrs Irwin:

> Don't get old dear; whatever you do, don't get old. It is nice to see you; it is nice to see anyone. I sit here by myself all the time. I see no one; I can't do anything. I've no one to talk to – the day is so long. I don't sleep well at night, so the

night is so long as well. Oh it is dreadful being old and not being able to get about, not being able to do anything all day It is so lonely being on your own.

The text of these interviews shows something of Mrs Irwin's isolation. It may not show, however, the pleasure that she gained from having a visitor. Her depression lifted during a visit and then her sense of humour would show through. She is not a naturally gregarious person and does not chat easily, yet she obviously gets great pleasure from quiet companionship. This form of simple friendliness is not easily given or taken from many of the visitors that call on her – the warden making hurried calls, the nurse on her rounds, the meals-on-wheels lady hurrying before the gravy congeals. Even her daughter's visit may be taken up with the practicalities of stocking the cupboards and sorting the clothes. Part of Mrs Irwin's depression comes from her awareness of her growing powerlessness, brought about by increased frailty. Frailty not only saps physical energy, it can sap the strength needed to renew your will to enjoy life. In this sense Mrs Foules has remained more robust, as her plans for Christmas show:

I'll be going to my niece's house on Christmas day and to my grand-nephew's on Boxing Day. Then there is the party at St Mary's on the Thursday before Christmas. There will be a 'do' at the Blue Centre on the Tuesday and then we will be going to the dinner for the people in these flats at the Orchard – that's on the Thursday after, I've paid for that already. I pay a bit every week all winter, the warden collects it for us.

Mrs Irwin sees Christmas differently:

I'm not looking forward to Christmas. It doesn't mean anything to someone like me, I can't get out to buy presents or anything. I expect I'll spend Christmas with one of my family, I don't know which; they will sort it out and one of them will come for me. I don't expect they will fight over having me, I'm such an old misery, no one wants an old misery at Christmas time, especially if there are children. My grandsons both have children, so they will want jollification, not an old misery. I can't join in any more, all I can do is sit. I used to be really jolly at Christmas and birthdays and things before I got miserable and helpless like I am now.

The slow smile that accompanied this shows that, despite the truth of what she is saying, Mrs Irwin is aware of the love of her family and sure enough of that to be able to laugh at herself.

Our purpose in putting these two interviews together is to show that despite society's tendency to respond in a uniform way to people who can be similarly categorised, people still remain individuals in old age, as at any time. In this chapter we meet two such individuals.

Mrs Foules

Have you lived in Loughborough all your life?

Yes, all my life. I know a bit about Loughborough!

What about your family?

None of them are alive, they're all dead. My mother and father and the eldest sister – she died about four years ago; my brother died about two years ago and my other sister, next to me, she died about 18 years ago. But her daughter is very good to me, my niece that is. That's her in the gilt frame. And that's her sister in Canada, that one, yes.

Does your niece still live in Loughborough?

Yes, she does. Oh, I should be lost without her, she comes down most days, she does my shopping – she's a very good help – and my washing. Does my washing now, I used to do it up to about three or four year ago, but it got a bit too much.

Do you still cook for yourself?

Yes, Oh! I cook and everything myself, yes, some of them have 'meals on wheels', but while I can do it I like to do it, it keeps you nimble.

What sort of things do you cook?

Oh! er, you know . . . lately it's been cabbage, carrots and the new potatoes I have now, but I think the peas are a bit dear yet. I find that when I do the peas I just eat them raw! When I'm shelling them, none ever end up in the saucepan. Well, that's how it used to be with me when they first come in especially. You know, you're shelling them and then you haven't got none when it comes to cook. But they are very dear. Last week I was at the Centre, I really enjoyed my dinner, because I go for my dinner you see. They come for Mrs Jones at the end bungalow, she goes as well; he comes about ten o'clock you see, and we go to the Centre at St Mary's.

Is that a Thursday you go?

Thursdays – so on Thursdays I'm always out now. We come back about three thirty in the afternoon, they do it voluntary, the man who fetches us. He's a very nice feller, he lives with his mother.

How long have you been going to St Mary's?

Just about 12 months, yes. Oh! I enjoy that, I really look forward to it. I used to go to Holy Cross Church – well the school-room adjoining. I used to go there but they're not so 'pally' as they are at St Mary's. There everybody knows you, Jane [the social worker] has got them to go at first. I won the raffle this week.

What did you win?

That was shortcake. Yes, I like that. We used to have it when we went to Scotland. I used to often go with my friend, but she died about five years now. You know, I didn't used to go until

I lost my husband you see. Then I had a letter from my friend 'cause she lived at Thurmaston, against Leicester, you know . . . Since, she got married and things changed; she went away and then when my husband died she wrote and said it would be nice to renew the friendship again – properly, if you're agreeable, she said. Oh! I soon wrote back and said, oh yes, it would be nice especially as I had lost my husband you see and . . . that year she wrote and says would you like to go to Scotland with me. So . . . I says I'd very much like to but I says, I don't want to come between you and your husband, I wrote and says, but she soon wrote back, 'You needn't worry about that, I've not been going with George for a long while. He got that mean he was too mean to spend the money and I thought (she went to work as well, you see) I wasn't going to miss my holiday.' So she used to leave him at home gardening – he enjoyed that more than going on holiday.

So what age were you when you went to Scotland the first time?

It must have been about 12 year ago. I had quite a few holidays with her in Scotland. Yes, it was very enjoyable; we got so we was like pals again.

So you kept in touch with your friend all through the years, did you?

Yes, right up till she died. Yes, she – we was the same age, yes and oh . . . I did miss her. 'Course, that finished going away for my holidays. Of course, I've not been to Scotland since, you see.

Do you get away for a holiday now?

Well, Jane has arranged for me to go this last two years to Glenfield, that's not far away you see, Glenfield with a Mrs Pullinger. I paid £55 a week, I used to go for a fortnight you see. I stayed there at her house, she took visitors in occasionally. 'Cause she was a widow, you see. I went with myself.

Did you enjoy it?

126

Yes, very much, yes, oh, yes. I'd been odd times with Mrs Smith – she's at the end bungalow – but since she's got in with that neighbour next to her . . . 'cause Mrs Eaton used to live next door and she died and then this one come from up Thorpe way.

How many bungalows are there along here?

Five. This is the middle one. There're two that side and two the other.

And do you know each other all very well?

Yes, pretty well, yes. We're all friendly all except that one, next to Mrs Jones, since she's come; she don't belong in the bungalows. Well, not after the other person that was there, she was very nice. She was really bed-ridden but she sat up in the chair, all day like, but she never went out, very rare – this new one! . . . I've never been very 'pally' with her, not like Mrs Jones, she's never out of there; I think Mrs Jones is frightened to tell her. She stops and stops, all day, and Mrs Jones daren't say nothing. When she's not in (Mrs Jones goes to her daughter's on a Tuesday generally), the other one thinks she can come in to me. I've had it a few times but I think, no, she's not going to make a 'makeshift' of me, so I can just see through the door with it being glass panel, I can just see who it is; so this last twice she come and knocked me thinking she'll come into me. She'll stop all the afternoon, oh, yes, she'll stop for tea. She's cheeky really.

And you don't like her to come?

No. She's not my type you know. And another thing she used to come to see me when Mrs Jones had gone to her daughter's and then she was calling her blue, calling her and yet she's there all the day, mostly; I can't do with anybody like that. So I thought well, I'm not going to go to the door. She kept knocking and knocking. I thought, no I'll have a rest and stop in. So then she shouts, she's had a stroke as well – 'course, I'm not going on about that, anybody who's been afflicted like that –

but she shouts. Oh, she shouts awful. Oh and she . . . there were something I said to her once. I was telling her off about something, 'cause I do tell her off sometimes. So I were telling her something and course she's always got this stick with her, she picked this stick up and I thought she was going to strike me really. She picked up her stick, 'Oh, I know I didn't, I know I didn't,' and I thought, oh, gracious, that stick's getting a bit near. So, I thought I'm not going to have her coming here many times with the stick.

Do you know many of the other people who live near here?

Oh yes, I go in to Mrs Thomas sometimes, she suffers with her legs really now. 'Course she's 94 she is. Her daughter comes most days and they take her out a lot; her daughter and her husband 'cause he's retired. She's only got the one daughter and she comes and does her cleaning for her: she doesn't have a home-help. I have a home-help come on Friday. Yes, she comes, nice girl.

Do you visit anybody else?

Oh, the lady at the bottom, she's very good. She comes in most nights if she gets home early enough, 'cause she goes to see to another old lady – she's 84, she lives by herself, we all live on our own, in these bungalows. But ever since that other one's come, she's upset the whole show. She has really, it never used to be like this, not like she is with her shouting . . . she'll say, 'Come and see me,' she often asks me to go to see her but I don't want to go to meet her again. So I think I've cured her of coming in, 'cause I would not go to the door, I made out I were resting, well, I was.

How long have you lived in this house?

Nearly 18 years next year. Well it might be getting on for 19, 'cause I'd been here for about a year when my husband died. We come from down against the Station Road. We lived there for about 50 years.

So your husband was retired when you came here?

Yes, yes, oh, yes and he'd been ill for 25 years with his eyes. He'd got conjunctivitis. He had to go up to, well, he used to go to Leicester to see Dr Curry, with the eyes and they'd never seen a case like it, 'cause the eyes swelled, the eyes swelled and come forward and they was inflamed as well. They said that they couldn't get down to it properly. So he had to go to Oxford. It was during the war. It may have been his job . . . he was a mechanic you know and that entails a lot of close work. He'd got blue eyes, you know and well, blue eyes are not so strong as the dark ones. They're on the weak side.

Was your husband able to go back to work?

No, he never went back. So he lived for 25 years like that; he used to have a shade on the left side – the one that burst its stitches. Then the other one could only be opened half-way, but he could see with that though; he had to have the dark glasses, but he lived 25 years after from when he had it done.

So what age was your husband when he died?

He was . . . let's see, he was . . . 77. That's nearly 18 years now.

Were you still working when your husband had the trouble with his eyes?

I was an overlocker then, making the garments up. We used to make trunks and under-vests and that sort of thing. 'Course, when I went to Leicester I opened out a lot more, I made children's wear and everything. I went to different factories, well, you had to. 'Cause if you got short one place, you'd got to look for another job. I worked there for about 30 years. I've done all sorts in hosiery. I've done children's wear, you know, the sets; legginettes and all that, in different places; in the hosiery I used to work in a factory that was in Loughborough where Lemyngton Street is now, but it got burned down. Well, you couldn't get any work; there were about 500 of us thrown out of work. They never started up again, and you'd got to look around, you couldn't get anything in Loughborough, they were all after different jobs and it was short time really for all the hosiery firms. I had to go to Leicester in the end, then you had to pay train fare, you see, or bus fare and that used to take your money for a start before you could say you were earning anything.

When did you stop working then, when did you retire?

I'd be 69 when I stopped. I kept on because my husband wasn't well. He was too ill for 25 years and never went to work and with him being only on the sick there wasn't much money. I was back in Loughborough then. Anyway, at the finish they wanted to put me back on me own time (piece work) and I had missed two years you see, and you miss your speed; I'd been two years on a set wage, you see. They were going to start put me back on me own time, so I says, 'Well, I've lost me speed now, I shan't earn much at that rate,' so I had a bit of an argument, I says, 'I'll think about it at the weekend.' But I didn't go back – after all, I was 69 by then. But I think they had a bit of a shock when I gave my notice in. 'Well,' I says, 'I'm not coming back on my own time, I've lost me speed,' and they expect you to go back as if you'd been on it all the while, no. Of course I could have gone to the union, but I didn't bother, I just left. I don't get any pension from them, but I get five pounds every Christmas.

Did you find it a big change when you left work?

Yes. Such a lot.

What did you miss most?

Oh! you miss the company. Me husband had been on to me to stop for a long while, he didn't like me going to work, but it was helping a bit with the money. But I soon found something to do all day, it did seem funny though when you had got the whole day. You see, I'd gone from a day at work to half-time, and that had got me partly used to it because I used to have to

get me jobs done then at home in between the half-days. So I'd
got a bit more time and when me husband wasn't so well, we
used to go out you see for walks. 'Cause he never liked to go by
his self.

Do you get out much now?

No. Not now, only to have me hair done. Oh and I go to the
Centre, when someone comes for me.

How long is it since you have been able to go out on your own?

Well it must be about five years or so. Yes, it must be. You
know I don't do my shopping now at all, my niece does that,
she's a good girl. I miss not being able to go out. But I'm pam-
pered when I do go out, 'cause they fetch me in the car you see; a
man, a voluntary worker he is. He takes Mrs Jones from that end
bungalow, we both go to St Mary's on a Thursday. But I do
manage to walk to the hairdressers I'm often late, more or less. I
go once a fortnight. Just to, well, I've been having it set, I've had
it set eight times, I've soon got to have it permed again.

*Would you ever walk down to the Orchard [the local pub] or
anything like that?*

Funny thing is, I go to the Orchard at Christmas for the dinner
and the warden's been this morning about that. She's putting
it down if we want to go. She says, 'I've come to see if you're
going to the Christmas dinner?' 'Oh,' I says, 'I think I will,
how much is it this year?' She says, 'Well, it's gone up.' It was
£3.10 last year – it's gone up to £4.20 this year. But they give
£2.15 towards it, the wardens, you see. She says you can pay so
much a week towards it and I said, 'I shall have to try and
manage that then.' So we're going again this year.

*Do you ever go down there in the evening for a drink or any-
thing?*

No, no. I think that the one that side, she often goes down, by
what they tell me, but it's very rare I see them with the curtains
drawn. I never bother once I've lit up, I never bother going

out. Sometimes I would go to Lizzie's house but not lately because Lizzie is never in now, she's looking after another old lady. She's getting on now. She was really bonny, she's really fat now, she can't get any shoes on now, it's awful. Her feet are swelling so. Mine are swelling a bit to what they used to be, a bit more you see, course this is due to water trouble. I have to take tablets for it, you know.

Are they painful?

Sometimes they are, worse at night, you know, so I don't sleep well at night. At least, not so well as I used to.

Do the nights seem long to you?

Oh yes, when you can't sleep very well they do. But you have to be thankful for small mercies. When you come to think, I'm nearly 90.

What time do you go to bed at?

Half past eleven which is quite late. It is really. Though I often have a nod here in between, but I used to go about ten o'clock but I got as if I used to lay awake, you know, thinking of everything. I thought I can't stick it so now I have the tele on quite a bit at night, and about eleven thirty I think it's about time I were getting ready for bed. So with going a bit later, I can sleep a bit better.

What time do you get up at then?

Sometimes, on a Thursday morning, that's when I've got to go to the Centre, I get up about seven thirty, else I get up about eight o'clock time. But I don't like to be late getting up really 'cause it throws you just that bit late but I do watch the clock more on a Thursday, I manage to get up about seven thirty then. I just gets me ready then. It'll be about ten o'clock when he comes for me with the car. He takes Mrs Jones and I in his car. We had a very nice dinner last week and do you know, it was only faggots we had for the meat but they were lovely faggots. I don't know where they'd had them from, what sort, I don't know whether they were Brains faggots, or any they'd had from the butchers up there, but they were really lovely and the gravy were lovely, smashing, better than the meat really. I enjoyed it – like they used to be. You seem to get the goodness you know in them last week, it were lovely. But we had faggots and mashed potatoes and some greens, cabbage.

What do you normally have for your lunch when you are home?

I have all sorts, put them all together in the saucepan, boil them up, it makes one, you can hot it up on the one thing, that's what I think about. I used to have it one, two or three lights, but not now, I do it altogether. It's not so expensive that way.

This morning I thought, well, I'll do the potatoes and I'll slice them up and then add a carrot and an onion, oh, the onions they aren't half strong. Made my eyes water they do. They are strong, I don't know where they are having them from but they've been dear lately. I had one a fortnight ago and it was 26p. Put them in them net bags, 26p for that. That was only a pound for 26p, but this week they'd gone down a bit – 16p. So it's a bit better. They're getting a bit cheaper but they are strong. Oh dear, talk about me eyes running. I were hoping nobody were coming I should have had to go to the door with my eyes running, I don't think it's done with me now, they keep watering. But I did enjoy it, I'd got potatoes boiled and a bit of carrot and an onion and then I'd got half a cabbage, put that in, so it all went in together and it was a lovely smell when it was doing. I think when you've got two or three lots like that, and you have an onion one onion seems to flavour it. Yes, lovely, I did enjoy it. I thought they're all going together.

Have you found your legs are all right for you to stand to prepare your lunch?

Yes, oh yes.

Mrs Irwin

Have you lived in this house very long?

17½ years, I think; I live rent-free now because I've paid for this flat. Well evidently I have because . . . I don't know, the council have just told me that I've no need to pay any more rent because I've bought it, I suppose that's how they mean it, I don't know, but I don't pay any rent.

How long have you lived in Loughborough?

I've lived in Loughborough since, now, my husband was working at Leicester . . . I've lived in Loughborough quite a while, wait a minute, I lost my first child, a boy, and then I had this one daughter, that's all, and I lived in William Street then, I think.

So it's a long time?

Oh yes, I've lived in Loughborough a long time. I like Loughborough a lot. There's good and bad everywhere. But I don't do so badly really, the only thing is that I'm so very lonely as I don't have visitors, that's the drawback.

Can you go out by yourself now?

Oh no, I've not been down the town for nearly two years, I wouldn't know what the shops are like. I used to have someone come and take me out in my chair, a wheelchair, they'd take me if they were capable enough, a girl about 18 or something like that. I don't think they're allowed to take the risk of taking me out in the wheelchair, under 18, I don't think so.

Did you like that, do you like going out in the chair?

Yes, because they could take me round the shops, like Tesco's, and I could see what I wanted, but nobody does that now. I haven't been out in my chair for a long, long time. No, I should like somebody to take me out really. It is a risk for them to take anybody like me, crossing the road. I understand it, that's one good thing about it, I do understand, but none the more for that I do regret not going out. I'm tired of being by myself, yes I am, I don't know what to do. I get up sometimes and pick up a duster and see a bit of dust somewhere and I think, oh I'll dust round, but I have to come and sit down so many times, oh dear, oh dear.

Do you read at all?

Oh yes. I've got a book there I'm reading. I think I've had that given to me. There's some more there, I have plenty of books. I like romances.

Would you do a bit of reading every day?

Oh yes, in fact I take a book to bed with me to get me to sleep. I don't sleep very well, I don't get much sleep. Well it stands to reason, I don't do anything to make me sleep, just sitting here, I very, very seldom sleep in the daytime, so I can't blame it on to that.

Does that mean the nights seem a bit long?

Yes, I wake up a lot of times, I've got trouble with my waterworks, I've been about eight times this morning, more than that I think . . . and I have to get up lots of times in the night.

Does that worry you, getting up in the night?

Well, no, not now it doesn't, because I've got used to it; if I don't wake up in the night I think I've gone into another world.

What time would you go to bed then?

Well round about – in between nine and ten – round about that time, I don't go to bed early, not too early. I've got my television, see. I've been watching the tennis, McEnroe, naughty boy. Now, I wouldn't have been watching that but my daughter told me watch the tennis and you'll get some excitement, so I just happened to put it on and it was him; he has been a naughty boy, hasn't he?

What about the morning, what time do you get up in the morning?

Sometimes I'm out here at six o'clock, not always, but sometimes I am, and if I want a cup of tea, if I want a drink, I generally come out and make myself a cup of tea; I drink tea and coffee.

And would you go back to bed again?

Oh no, once I've got up I don't never go back to bed, unless I feel really ill, though I don't think I'd go back to bed if I was really ill because I'd sooner sit here, if I'm going to die I'll sit in my chair and die.

Do you manage to get yourself dressed?

Yes, it's a bit hard though, I put one thing on and sit down, and put another thing on and sit down. I don't do so bad for myself, really, it's a case of having to, really. Still I am 90, you know. So it's time I went really, isn't it, when you come to think of it. Of course I used to have a home help some time after I'd lost my husband, I wish I had one more regularly than I do now. I never had one at all last week, not a soul, only my daughter on Tuesday. I wish my husband had been here a bit longer. That's all my family on there, those photographs.

So your daughter comes to visit you on Tuesdays?

Yes, because her husband has his day off from business then, you see. She doesn't drive, but of course he's got a car for his business and that's his day off so they generally spend as long as they can. He brings her over, she generally brings me a lot of grocery stuff, you see, she keeps me well stocked up.

Have you any other children?

I've got grandchildren, two grandsons, there's all my family on there. I should like to see them more often but of course they can't come when they're at business, naturally enough.

The girls don't drive so they can't come on their own, but they do come and see me now and again. I don't have to ask them, they come when they can, so it's nice to see them. And they're having babies, the young ones are. They've got beautiful homes, my two grandsons, and they keep improving on them, they're getting on, they don't stand still, they seem to be getting much more money every time and buying, they've got beautiful homes.

Have you been to their homes?

Yes, they have fetched me, perhaps for one of the children's birthdays, or something like that. But they don't fetch me too often, not often enough, they haven't time, you see. No, I understand that, they've got their own homes to see to and their own children to bring up, so I don't expect too much from them, it's very nice of them to do what they do do. I've got no regrets as regards my family.

Have you any brothers or sisters?

Oh yes, I've got a sister in London. She's phoned me and told me that she's coming to see me, I think, but she's eighty something and she can't travel on her own, she has to bring somebody with her. She said can I put her up? I can put you up all right, you come and see me, I'd sleep on the floor to see her, I wouldn't mind. Although I haven't told her that because she wouldn't come if she thought I was going to sleep on the floor. I said we shall manage, I've got the settee here, it takes two people, and the bedclothes and everything so I wouldn't have to bother about that, but she can't travel on her own.

How long is it since you last saw her?

I can't remember, dear.

A couple of years, or more than that?

More than that, it's a long time since she came here. She lives in Bush Hill Park in London. She phones me occasionally but if she's going out for a holiday when she is coming back, she tells me that, I suppose her life is not very interesting for her to keep phoning me.

Do you ever write to her?

I don't write letters now. I've never written many letters, really. Well of course there's so many of these cards now where they can say what they want to say, can't they . . . and then I have the phone. My daughter phones me every day. Round about eleven o'clock. She rings me every day. She asks me what I'm doing and what I've done and what I've eaten during the day, have I had a meal, did I have any breakfast, did I do this and did I do that, and she tells me what to do. Yes, she tells me what to do. What have you had for your breakfast? And I say to her, 'Not much, I've had a cup of tea.' 'Haven't you had anything to eat?' See, this is how she talks to me so it's a good job I've got somebody like that. Well, there is the warden – she lives in the next block, upstairs, and she phones me every morning to ask how I am. She'll call if she thinks I'm not very well. She'll come in and see me, because she's got two or three people in this block that she comes to see, although of course she can't stay long, she'd have too much to do, but I think there's more people that she has to come to in this block than any of the blocks. I don't ask her to get me anything. I suppose she would, but I don't know whether she would, you see, because if it was known that she did for me, others would want it, naturally enough, so I'm afraid that if I asked her to get anything she wouldn't do again because if the others knew she'd got me something, do you understand me? I want bread now and I've not known how to get it, there's nobody I could ask, my neighbour next door, she's on her holidays, but she won't get me anything . . . Shops don't deliver now, do they? I don't know. I've never had a shop deliver me anything up till now. Still I suppose they would if they knew me. I don't know them you see. I knew them when Mr Newman had the shop; if he'd have been there they would probably have done. His shop was next to the fish and chip shop. I often fancy a bit of fish and chips at night, I love fish, but there's nobody here to get it for me. I did ask one of the children that was playing out here once if she'd go down and she did, but it cost me as much as the fish and chips for her to go because I can't ask them to go without giving them money. And I love fish and chips. It would often be a meal for me.

Do you know many of the other people in the flats?

No, because they either die off or they go into hospital. In this block they put all the invalids in I think, down below, yes, they're all on the ground floor. Most of the retired are down below, on the ground floor. Upstairs now they're putting young people with children in. Why they do all that kind of thing we don't know, because people underneath complain about it, nobody else has children above them. It's so funny that the council pick on this block of flats for all the – well, nuisances, I should say.

A younger woman than me lives next door, she's on her holiday. She's gone down to her daughter in Kent, she said they pick on this place to put all the rubbish, that's what she says, rubbish in these flats, and they seem to do that. And just lately they've put people with children upstairs, young children, they run along the passage, you can hear them. There's one elderly person she's giving up her flat to go into hospital sooner than live here. She's going into hospital, she can't stand it. Well, you can't do with it when you're old, you can't do with people running about over your head, really, children screaming, and doing that kind of thing. I know they've got to go about but the parents won't allow them to come down here because they can't see them, so I don't know, I'm sure. Yes. I don't think there's anybody happy in this block. No I don't. I'm sure you'll find people – well, I don't think there's anybody as old as me down below, but they are elderly and they have to stay indoors so I don't know how they stand the children running about. You'll have to excuse me, I've got to go to the toilet.

Where did you get the walking frame from? Did the social worker bring it to you?

Yes, one of the social workers, yes. But it is broken, it doesn't go straight, you see. It needs to be fixed. I don't know who to phone to, I don't know who it is. I shall have to find out, you see. I haven't made a fuss about it. It's only to get about the house . . . I had one with . . . well it's out there isn't it . . . one without the wheels, but my shoulders got that sore lifting it up to walk.

Do you generally keep fairly well?

Well, yes, just as I am now.

Do you see the doctor often?

Oh yes, she comes pretty regularly. I have a lady doctor now. I like the lady doctor, she's very nice, really, well I like the lady doctor because she has to look at me, in between my groin and under my breast it's all practically raw, and I didn't like the idea of letting the doctor see me really, so she's very nice. I think she's old-fashioned, if you know what I mean, whether it is that she couldn't afford clothes, but she dressed old-fashioned, but she's very, very nice, she's a mother to me, if you understand what I mean, like a mother. You see I don't mind her looking at me and I should hate a man to see.

How long have you had the lady doctor?

Well, not long because she's not been with them long; you see, there's been four men doctors. They didn't get a lady doctor just for me, but when I heard that they'd got a lady doctor I asked if I could transfer to her and she was quite nice. She comes to me now occasionally when I have to send for her. She came about three weeks ago, and I take all that stuff.

What do you take all these for?

The tablets are for my water, and I've got heart tablets, I've got cream as I'm always sore under my breasts, always, red raw sometimes, and I have to put cream on then, and of course them white tablets there, you can see. I generally put them out first thing in the morning for the day so that I know what I've taken. It's quite difficult to keep count sometimes so I generally amuse myself and put them out for the week, Sunday to the next following Sunday; Sunday to Sunday, I should say.

Are you worried about your health? Are you ever worried that you might get ill?

No, no I don't, because I expect it, you see, at my age. I expect these things; in fact some old ladies are worse off than I am, in a sense. Really, it is that I can't get about, that's the only thing, and I don't have anybody. I'm *lonely*, and I think being lonely is a kind of illness – it's a drawback at any rate. I don't see a soul all week, until I have my home help on Friday, and then they only allow me to have her for two hours.

Do you ever get meals on wheels?

Yes, they bring me – they have started bringing me meals on wheels – they've only just started to do this – the days I don't go out they bring them. I'm all right for meals. But they don't get a chance to stop because they've got other people's meals to take as well, you see, there's two or three along here I think have meals on wheels, it's lovely and hot and I could eat it directly they bring it but it's sometimes about eleven o'clock, sometimes it's about quarter to twelve – all times, it's all according how they get round. Still I'm grateful. I have to pay for all this, you see, out of my pension. Excuse me for saying this, I never get anything for nothing.

How much do you have to pay for your meals on wheels?

[Mrs Irwin starts to look in her bag for the ticket. She pulls one out] Oh, that's Harrington Court, I even have to pay to go there. £1.25 every week – that's for my lunch. I haven't been there this week because I haven't been too good. There are women like myself there – they are all elderly women. They come and fetch me – they are all very nice . . . Yes, somebody comes in a car. I suppose he gets paid for fetching us, so really and truly I don't get anything for nothing, if you understand

141

me, and I'd far rather pay for it while I can. You're not under an obligation then are you?

On Thursdays I go to St Mary's for the day. They come about eleven o'clock, we play cards or dominoes or something like that. It's quite enjoyable and they're people like myself, some are worse than others, so it's quite enjoyable really, those two days, Harrington Court and St Mary's. Really and truly I've got nothing to complain about.

Do you think you'd like to live in a home where you'd be with others all day?

Well, I don't know, I have been in a . . . I don't know where it is now, I've been twice, where there's been people, they could stay in bed if they wanted, and it's been nice. Twice I've been in and I've really enjoyed it.

And have you arranged for another visit?

Well, nobody's asked me or anything or approached me about it really. Yes, I've been twice for a fortnight, but I can't tell you where I've been. Twice I've been and I've come out a lot better than when I went in. Because I've stayed there for a fortnight, of course they've kept my pension, naturally enough, well it's only natural, and my daughter could come and see me there you see. It's awful I can't think where it is.

Would you like to do that again, go in for another short while?

Yes, I wouldn't mind. I wouldn't mind going again really. But I'm glad when I get home. I could have stayed there, but I didn't want to – not until I was right forced to. I don't like the, what do you call it, oh dear oh dear, the sameness of the thing, you know you have to wash at certain times, you have to do this, you have to do that.

The routine?

The routine, yes, I couldn't think of the word, I wouldn't like that. Here I can do as I like. Yes, so I'm going to stay here as long as I can, of course.

142

[The next time we called, Mrs Irwin was reading] I'll just put my book down. I've had it given me. Margaret Powell, *Below Stairs*. It's rather nice. She was in service and she knows all about that kind of life.

It's not the type of work you ever did, is it?

Oh, I wasn't in service, no, but I used to go out working. Yes dear.

Where did you go out to work?

Well I'd go out to ... go out and work for elderly people! [Laughter] Well, I say nobody comes and works for me, but they do. Only once, on a Friday, that's all. Two hours on a Friday – a home help – she came yesterday. I know her because she has been before. Yes. And she's a good worker. You know, she works while she talks. She don't leave off work. She does it very good, as if she were doing her own, that is, if you understand what I mean. Yes. But she's only coming for the regular one, because she's on holiday you see.

So – have you been doing anything since I saw you last?

Yes – just sitting in my room as usual, just here. No, I haven't been anywhere in particular. But I will do during the summer: they're trying to persuade me to go somewhere for a fortnight. Somewhere. But – it's very nice, I've been before, I went last year. Very nice. But I was glad to come home, that's it.

Who is it who is trying to persuade you?

Well, I don't know dear, I don't know them really. They're whatsername people, like – well I don't know.

Social services?

Yes. That's it. And they're ever so nice about it. I mean, they don't make a fuss if I refuse. Although I don't – up to now I haven't refused. Because it's been a break for me to get away from here, sitting like this all day long.

Whenever you're sitting like that all on your own, what do you think about?

Well – I think about dying, to tell you the truth. It doesn't worry me. Because of my age, you see. It doesn't worry me because I'm ready to go any day. I don't mind. I shan't mind. I'm not worried about dying, I've lived my life. Well when you get to 90 . . . So I've lived my life. And I don't like living like this, because I've always been, you know, able to do my work and been up, and I've been out to work as well. And I've worked for other people. So I don't like living like this. But still. It's a case of having to, that's the point. I can't do anything else about it. I mean, I can't go without taking this walking frame with me all the time I get up. I go out to make myself a cup of tea, I have to take that with me, you see. Because if I fall down, the point is – I may not fall down, but if I fall down, there's nobody here to pick me up and I wouldn't be able to get up, you see, because my legs wouldn't let me. I should have to lie there and crawl . . . I've often wondered what I should do, to tell you the truth. And I thought to myself, say I fell in the kitchen when I go to makė myself a cup of tea, I should have to kind of crawl to the warden, to the alarm, you see. And she'd have to come and pick me up, because it would be impossible for me to get up. I haven't fallen down yet, touch wood.

Is that something that worries you?

Well, yes. It worries me to have to call on somebody like that, you see. Though she's very, very nice. Very nice. But I should have to call on somebody to pick me up off the floor, and I can't do it myself, that's what annoys me. Well – annoys me – it worries me, it doesn't annoy me. Because I know sometime that I might do. I mean I might kick up a mat or a carpet or something like that, you see. But I've warned them . . . when I've talked about it, they say, well you shouldn't have them on the floor, then. Oh Lord, I couldn't have that, bare floors. I couldn't. I couldn't have bare floors, so.

It's nice to know that the warden is there?

Oh yes. She would come. I don't make a nuisance of myself – well, I hope I don't. No, I don't make a nuisance of myself. I've never called on her yet. She just calls me in the morning to see if I'm all right, and I say yes, I'm all right. And if I needed her during the day, because I've been . . . well, I haven't fell down yet actually. So if I needed her she would come directly, you know, she wouldn't make no fuss about it. She only lives in the next block you see. Was it you that took me out?

Yes it was.

Took me out shopping? Well, go on! Didn't we have a lovely time, oh I keep on looking back at that, that was a lovely, that was a lovely day.

You met quite a few people too, didn't you. You knew the girl in the paper shop.

Oh yes. Well I've always dealt there, you see, when I was well enough to get about. Always. And she is a friend of my daughter's, you see. She's my daughter's age. Yes she knew me. It's been a long time since I've been able to go down town. When my husband was alive we used to go out together you see. Well he's been gone – he just lived here a year after we moved in here. Just a year, that's all. And I've been here 17 years now. So it's 16 years ago he died. We didn't have any other children. We had two – we had one girl, and we lost a boy. We had two children. That's the family on there. Great-grandchildren, yes. Yes. It's nice – when I do a bit of dusting, I have a little talk to them. Yes. [Laughter] Don't see them very often, but still. Because they're outside, you see, they're not in the town at all.

Whenever you look back over all your 90 years, what do you think of as being your happiest times?

When my husband was alive. Naturally. We never went anywhere without one another. Never. He was a Loughborough man. But he came on munitions when the war was on you see. And I worked in the same factory as him you see. I was on a machine, and he used to come and do my machine when anything went wrong, you see. Yes. And we got married in London. I think back about it quite a lot now. Yes I do. I used to make shells as big as this table, but I only did the heads you know, the screwed-on sort. I stopped work when the war ended, when the children were born. I had a son and a daughter. I lost my son – seven years old he was. He died in Guy's Hospital; my husband and I, we used to go up there at the weekends. We had the daughter after when we came back and everything was all right. That's all we had. Two children and a dog.

Did you ever go back to work whenever you lived in Loughborough? After your daughter was born?

I don't think so. I can't remember, dear. I can't remember. No. Isn't it funny. There are some parts of your life that you forget, you know. Yes, well really and truly, I could write a book on my life from the time I was able to write. I know it wouldn't be very exciting I don't suppose for other people, but it would be for me to look back on, in a way, because I forget quite a lot now. I forget a lot of things now. Forget how to lay my money out properly – for the things I need to spend it on. I wonder how to do it . . . I only have my pension, I don't have another penny. I haven't any money at all. I've never have had money, not to have money to spare, kind of thing.

Is your pension enough?

Well, it just does it – I just manage – especially now, because there's not much to buy that costs much – that costs anything for me to eat. My daughter keeps me well stored up with tins of soup and things like that – you only have to look in the cupboard to see what she does on a Tuesday. She fills us up there and then I live on that. Otherwise I wouldn't be able to live on my pension. At any rate I don't enjoy my food now. No I don't enjoy anything really. The only thing I enjoy is a cup of tea. Really, more or less. And I don't sometimes enjoy that.

146

This is lemonade. I don't know why I don't enjoy food. Because I don't work for it, I suppose, that's about it.

Well you worked for your pension, didn't you?

Oh yes, I worked for my pension, yes, but I've had a pension for a long, long time. And it don't go very far now, really. Still I manage on it, so . . . I don't go out to spend it.

That's a very smart jumper you've got on. I like that colour

Yes, everybody tells me that when I go out. I wear it under my coat. Everybody remarks about it, and I've had it years. I've never bought an article of clothing since I've been – well, since I've been indoors, you know, as the saying goes. Not even an apron, so all the clothes I've got I've had years. I've got four of those trousers and coats. All different. And when I go to whatsername House – because I don't remember exactly – they say, my name's Laura you see, and when I go in, 'Oh, here comes our Laura!' You know, it sounds so nice. They say, 'Oh, she's got another coat on!' I've got four and they're all different colours. The brown I wear with the brown trousers and I've got a blue that I wear with the blue trousers so whether they think I've just bought these things I don't know. But I've had them for years! I don't need clothes. No. No, I don't need any clothes at all really.

Do you watch much television?

Well no, I don't really. I get fed up with it you see. That's the point. No I don't watch much of it. I get down to watching it in the evening, you know, the two serials; *Coronation Street* and the other one, *Crossroads*. I generally watch them. If I think about it.

Do you watch the News?

Oh yes, yes. I nearly always keep up with the News. I get the newspaper every day, a lady upstairs puts hers through the door for me, so I do very well. I'm very, very lucky. I know she's put it through the door, because you hear the, you know, hear the box go up. But no, I don't have the television on much, oh no. I don't, because I hear the man upstairs, he has his on. He's at home all day; his wife goes to work, she's semi-blind, and he's at home, takes the dog out for a walk, two or three times a day, that's all, and that's all the work he does. You never hear a broom put on the floor, you never hear any cleaning done. I'd like to go and find out what it's like, no, you never hear any cleaning done. I can hear their television, or sometimes it's some music. He's a pest with it really. His wife, she's semi-blind, she goes to work. Well I think she's nearly blind any road, but he lives on her, ever since he's been here he's never done a day's work, never, don't do any work at all, so where he gets his money from I don't know. Still, good luck to him, there's a lot more like him, so he's not alone. Still they don't keep the T V on too late. But some days he has it on all day long and some days I don't hear it at all. But I think he goes somewhere, some other lady's house. I'm surmising now, aren't I?

Do you like a little bit of gossip?

No, not about other people's lives. To be quite candid I'm a poor neighbour to him because I can't gossip, well I don't want to know their lives, if you know what I mean, because I've got quite enough to do with my own to bother about other people's. I suppose that's what makes me so lonely really, it's my own fault.

Are you interested in politics at all?

No, dear. No I'm not. I just like to know what's going on in the world, yes, I do, yes. I'm . . . [she started to laugh]

What are you laughing about?

Trying to remember what I am! I'm a . . . my family was er . . . oh dear. What's the different names?

The parties do you mean?

My family were always Labour, that's right. Yes.

148

And did you vote?

Yes.

Do you usually vote now?

No – unless they come and fetch me. I do vote if they come and fetch me. And they nearly always do, really. Yes. Up at the school . . . I still vote Labour. I don't think much of Mrs Thatcher as Prime Minister. I think she's too – well I think that she's got herself into trouble, hasn't she. [Looking at the newspaper] What it says is . . . she's just got herself into trouble, they're beginning to dislike her, aren't they? She's too bigoted. Too full of her own importance. I've always been against a woman being a head of the . . . I think it's a man's job. I think so, any road. I don't say everybody thinks like me, but they wouldn't or they wouldn't have voted for a woman, natural enough. Now I've always had the feeling it should be a man's job.

The things that women do nowadays are very different from what they did . . .

Oh years ago, it's true. Yes. Well – er – well I don't know really, I'm not interested in that. Not so very interested in politics anyway.

What about other sorts of things like going out to work, being educated and having careers. Do you think it a good thing, for women to do that?

No I don't. I don't really. I don't know why. It's perhaps because I never had a position of my own, that's about it. You see I've never been very forceful as regards the position I've been in, you see. Probably that's it. Probably. I don't know if it is. Yes, very likely. Because when I was brought up it was just men then, you see.

13
Reflections

The context of old age

All of us throughout our lives need and search for personal fulfilment, self-respect and security. However, the ways in which such goals are achieved in youth or middle-age may be very different from the ways used in old age. Furthermore, these goals can be achieved far more easily earlier in our lives than later when the structures and relationships that routinely aid us are less available.

In Britain, as in many western societies, security, independence and a sense of worth frequently come from employment. People use knowledge about another person's job to judge and accord them prestige and interest. But these 'supports' do not last once one's working life is over, so new ways have to be found to realise the goals and needs that still remain. Of course, many women now over 60 have never worked, except perhaps briefly before marriage or during the wars. Even those who did work often had lower status jobs that provided little financial security and less fulfilment than that available to men. As a consequence many working women have always been dependent upon their husbands or families for material support and status.

For women who have not had paid employment family relationships are often the sole source of financial and emotional security, a situation that at least historically has been supported by law. Caring for the family is an important source of fulfilment for many women and is sometimes their only way of exercising power.

Relationships with others, particularly with partners and immediate family, are an important source of purpose and value for everyone. Despite frequent irritations, most people need the companionship and shared responsibilities of joint living. But here again the old can lose out as spouses and close friends die and new relationships become hard to establish. In Britain today three out of every four women over 70 live alone.

What we find then is that many women reach pensionable age having spent their lives financially and emotionally dependent upon others, and it is precisely in these later years that they have to face and respond to enormous changes, perhaps bigger than any they have ever confronted before. Like men, they have to devise ways of creating and maintaining a sense of purpose and worth that is not dependent on work, either their own or that of their partner. But increasingly, they are likely to have to face these changes and new experiences alone.

You think that going from school to work is a big thing, but then you've got so much confidence that you sail through it. Retiring is by far the hardest thing I have ever faced.

The challenge of old age

These then are the goals of the old women we interviewed: to strike a balance between the need for security and the need for independence and self-respect; to ensure that a life of 'non-work' is made meaningful and leisure is both valued and seen as legitimate. Achieving these goals is difficult in itself, and further complicated by having to challenge the ageism in society, that attitudes that see you as 'old' before you feel you are old.

Life's pleasures change as circumstances change. Mrs Patel still loves the noise and laughter her grandchildren bring, but

Mrs Harman now prefers the company of people her own age who can talk about the same things. What becomes important is being able to go out and see others, being fit enough to join in activities that provide interest, companionship, and an opportunity to contribute and belong. Miss Moss enjoys the pleasure of not having to get up in the morning; Mrs Wates craves activities so she goes to the Ladies Circle, the Over 60s, a keep-fit class, plays bridge and goes to the library; Miss Stewart loves her telly, especially the afternoon soap operas. When talking about what it was they were seeking from old age the women used phrases such as, 'having some pleasure', 'peace', 'meeting people', 'enjoyment', 'pleasing myself', 'not having to fight'.

As we see in the interviews these women work hard to construct a satisfactory life for themselves. But what is also apparent is that the relationship between the various needs in their lives is a complex one. Status, self-respect, and interest come from interacting with others in a way that conveys a sense of value and enjoyment. These activities also give a sense of personal control and choice. Age and physical decline often threaten the continuation of these activities and friendships, and heighten a need for security. But as women grow older, in our society at least, security generally means surrendering some personal control and initiative. They know that inevitably this will reduce their independence. Every interview provides evidence of these tensions, of the need to seek a balance between security and independence either in the present or the future.

Mrs Hatter is well cared for in her old people's home but she can no longer decide things as small as when to get up, or what to eat, or when to receive visitors, even though she is quite capable of making such choices. Mrs Hatch still lives on her own but her poor mobility means that she is dependent on her daughter to take her shopping and to visit all but her immediately adjacent friends. She's lost considerable initiative in her life, but she has a stronger sense that people are on hand to help her if she needs them. That is an important anxiety removed. Maggie has no one she can turn to for that type of reassurance. Although she has perhaps the greatest drive to maintain control over her life, she would give anything to know that there was some security for her very old age from children or grandchildren. Mrs Irwin fears that one day she will fall in her kitchen and not be able to get up, but nevertheless is prepared to take this chance and carry on looking after herself because that way she can please herself. Individual women may resolve the conflicting demands in different ways, but all the women face the same issue.

These tensions between independence and security are most clearly illustrated by relationships within the family which remains the major source of security for old women. Only one woman we interviewed was living with her family, although several more of them had moved nearer to relatives since becoming pensioners. Many of the women received regular help from their relatives and recognised their dependence on them. These same women often recognise the dangers in their situation, and have ambivalent attitudes towards accepting help and increasing their dependence because it could lead to a 'drawing in' and 'giving up'. Many women tried to control quite tightly what help they would take, sometimes even accepting loneliness rather than a loss of independence. While guarding against such a situation, most of the women did however take great pleasure in their families and enjoyed the time with them. One weekend Mrs Hatch moved into her daughter's home to stay with her two teenage grandsons while their parents were away. They played darts together, watched the television and she organised the meals. Just for a while she was back in a familiar, and much missed role, and they all enjoyed the time together. Miss Moss writes to all her nieces and nephews and takes pleasure in seeing them grow and establish independent relationships with her. Mrs Hatter can't wait for her niece to come and take her to her home and garden for the day. Family photos hang on almost all the walls and the women told us many stories about the different people. Photos are also memories, usually happy ones, and a constant reminder of enjoyable times.

Just a few of the women, however, resented their families because they felt they had been unjustly labelled as incompetent or as a problem. Freda was hurt by them telling her what to do, and the implication that she could not look after herself properly was very painful for her. Mrs Hatter could not understand why she had had to leave her daughter and son-in-law, because 'I'd never got in the way. I kept myself to myself and never stopped them going out.' Mrs Ghandi's severed relationship with her family stemmed not from issues associated with her age, but from her challenging the division of labour in the household. The separation from her husband, however, has left her isolated and rejected by her family in her old age. Rarely, if at all, had these women protested to those involved about their treatment, or revealed the hurt. This apparent acceptance of pain and rejection is discussed later on.

For many pensioners the issue of dependence is one that only looms gradually. A more immediate problem is to confront the inevitable labelling that comes with the receipt of a pension. Many of those in their sixties and seventies do not think of themselves as old, yet they are constantly faced with attitudes that demean them and threaten their sense of worth. The interviews are full of examples of this, although the women do not always express it in these terms. One who did is Mrs Pullan, who is certain that the hostility of the young around where she lives is directed specifically at the old. Their lack of respect in the form of noise, foul language, and physical intimidation is felt and hurts her and the other residents. Kate tackled a group of youths whose presence near her flat was intimidating, and rounded on them when they swore at her. The rest of the women report without comment daily reminders of their low status; few people stop to help them across the road, bikes are thrown down in front of them, people do not move over on the pavements, conversations about personal matters are conducted in the public dining-room for all to hear, and cleaners enter rooms without knocking.

Some of the women also experience the double fear of being old and a woman. This prevents them from getting out alone, particularly at night, and increases their unease on the streets and in their homes. Many said they stayed in unless they were certain that someone would walk or drive them home. Such fears can curtail their activities and increase the extent to which they have to seek help.

A further example of how our society tends to denigrate old age is the way in which the everyday actions of the old are interpreted, and thereby reinforce the stereotypes. Thus stiff old women slowly crossing the road are seen as a nuisance, a danger to themselves and others; pensioners taking time to shop carefully from a very low income are seen as holding up busy modern workers juggling home, job and family. How often is the more accurate picture seen or understood? A picture of women keeping themselves active, caring for themselves and others, with every right to be out and about, and in no sense making illegitimate or unreasonable demands.

Meeting the challenge

What were the different responses of the women we interviewed to the challenges of old age?

One of the greatest contrasts we found in talking to these women was between the evidence for ageism, that all of them mentioned, and their apparent acceptance of it. Here then we have a group of women, facing disadvantage from a number of different quarters, but apparently unmoved by it or oblivious to it, although, as we shall argue below, lack of recognition does not preclude them from fighting it day in and day out.

How can we account for this apparent lack of anger? It is perhaps best explained as a result of several pressures, not least of which might be self-protection. In the first chapter we suggested that it can be difficult for a person needing help to confront the provider of care in an overt manner because of the fear that services will be removed. This suggestion is borne out in a number of the discussions. Such a fear lay behind the refusal of one woman to be interviewed; the anxiety that some critical assessment of the way she felt she was treated would be found out and used against her. Her friend in the home, Mrs Hatter, was more forthright but often broke off and dropped her voice to a whisper. Freda never spoke against her family's interventions even though she resented them, because she wanted a quiet life. Caught in a web of needs, and increasingly unable to meet them alone, silence may seem the only choice.

A further reason for the lack of anger may be that women have little consciousness of the ageism they face. The interviews showed a limited critique of their own position, frequently accompanied by a denial of their interest in politics. Even the few with active political involvement expressed little awareness of society's discrimination against the old and adopted an apolitical stance towards ageism. This is not really surprising, as the very pervasiveness of ageist attitudes means that they are more difficult to identify and target. The poor standard of provision of services, pensions, housing, etc., provoked more comment, although again in terms of an individual's position, not as part of a coherent political approach. This lack of a consciousness of the systematic nature of their disadvantage is all the more likely in a society that does not see old age in political terms or the elderly as a political resource. Thus if there are women who identify and articulate the nature of the world they face, or question why they are treated in ways they find inappropriate, few organisations or institutional structures come forward to support them. Any actions or protests remain individual and easily deflected.

It would be a mistake to assume that this lack of critique or political involvement implies a lack of response. Irrespective of the degree to which ageism is recognised we can see a common response from these women. Confrontations and disappointments are explained away or excused as the acts of a few, leaving most of society in the clear. Mrs Wates, longing to hear from her daughter more regularly, excuses her by saying that she works and has her housework to do as well as needing some time to herself. Mrs Hatch discounts the noisy, unruly children that are sometimes a nuisance because that's the way young people are; they've got their own ways of doing things. Miss Moss thinks that perhaps a move to another area, nearer her niece, might increase her sense of social ease and acceptance because there she is likely to come into contact with more professional people. Occasionally, the responsibility for the rebuffs is attributed to the old themselves. Maggie says you can see older women 'tightening their lips', and several of them talk of those they know who moan and grumble all the time so that it's not surprising that others ignore them or are sharp with them.

The pattern of response that we have identified is therefore one that contains a degree of generosity towards other people that the old themselves seldom receive. None the less this must not be equated with passivity and lack of challenge. Once we begin to look at how these women live and spend their time, against a background of what they face, the persistent challenge on their part becomes clearer. Faced with few resources, declining health and mobility, the loss of partners and friends, and the threat if not the actuality of increased dependence, most fight all the time to retain control and initiative, and accordingly they have lives that they find pleasurable and satisfying for much of the time. Nevertheless, the fight is not unlike a guerilla war: unannounced, unacknowledged, small-scale and relentless. It has been said by one writer that she sees in the lives of old women a 'daily heroism . . . a depth of survival knowledge, . . often a special inventiveness and creativity'. (Rich)

This inventiveness and creativity can be seen in all the interviews recorded here. Although they are often in pain, the women go out to ensure they stay as mobile as possible. They cross roads, even if others do not stop and help them; they climb perilously steep bus steps, often watched by others, and risk falling, in order to go to town for a day out. They search for better places to live, and move house. They learn to drive to maintain mobility. Many had taken up new activities as they aged – visiting places, joining a course – and several of the women explicitly said that activities were an important way of

157

staving off further decline, both physical and social. There is an inevitable drawing in but a lot of evidence that it is fought. There are challenges against the acceptance of services for the old, and the expectations or wishes of kin. Some refused meals on wheels, preferring to cook for themselves; some refused to give up their homes and move in with relatives while they were able to care for themselves. Sometimes the challenges are less visible. Mrs Hatter takes her water tablet from the orderly every morning and then puts it down the sink because she doesn't need it.

Survival tactics are equally varied and inventive. Mrs Stewart had a system for communicating with her niece about whether or not she had read a particular library book. Maggie could reach everything she needed with a system of strings and sticks. More fundamentally, many of the women had survival strategies for loneliness, for dealing with the pain of isolation and the depression that was often near the surface. Survival strategies help you to cope, but they don't remove these emotions. Hence Mrs Hatch still needed to cry, to let the loneliness come out and pass, but she had learnt to keep her pride and dignity by making this a private experience. Mrs Pullan needed help to counter her declining confidence and sense of loss of purpose and found it in a migraine support group and a relaxation programme. Mrs Patel kept herself busy; Miss Moss liked to have appointments in her diary; Ruby continued working as a way of getting out. Reflections about the past, a sense of oneness with their deceased husbands, was for some a survival strategy; sometimes these memories were allocated a special part of the day, as with Mrs Hatter or Mrs Irwin, a part of the day that gave them particular pleasure.

Summing up

Being old and a woman is to be in a complex and difficult situation. Women face considerable personal readjustment as they age, most notably the balance between independence and

158

security, which has to be achieved within the context of a prejudiced world. They may not realise the systematic nature of the ageism they experience, but this does not alter the fact that they confront it daily and devise ways to keep control and initiative. Their challenges, however, are individual and dependent on whatever strength they can find. The physical and social forces limiting such challenges become progressively stronger.

At the moment each generation of older women faces the same issues anew without preparation or support. Each struggles independently to deal with the situations they face, looking to each other for companionship. Unless old age becomes an issue that other groups raise, there seems little likelihood that the position of older women will change in any way in the near future. The attitudes of the young, as well as the nature and distribution of resources, has to be challenged in order to remove the discrimination and disadvantages.

> Ageism can be seen as a process of systematic stereotyping of and discrimination against people because they are old, just as racism and sexism accomplish this with skin colour and gender. Old people are categorised as senile, rigid in thought and manner, old-fashioned in morality and skills . . . Ageism allows the younger generation to see old people as different to themselves; they subtly cease to identify with their elders as human beings.[10]

Old age has to be politicised, and become an issue of importance and knowledge to those not yet old. The position adopted by the political parties is characterised by little interest or action with regard to older people. However, some interest has recently been expressed by socialist groups with the publication of radical manifestos for old age (see for example Bornat, Phillipson and Ward[11]). Other political groups, such as those linked with the women's movement, have to date shown little interest in the position or experiences of older women.

So far the women's movement has resonated with its silence

on the subject of the status of old women. As if our old women were indeed too depressing for us, or an embarrassment to us, or beyond the reach of our feminist analysis. Even when we have sought out an old woman for her oral history . . . we have shown notably little interest in the challenges of her life today as an aging woman.[12]

This was written about America but the position in Britain seems little different. One important first step has been to challenge our own ageism and find out from older women what it is like to be old. Without the deliberate creation of opportunities for older women to speak, they are unlikely to be heard. Not because older women lack opinions and thoughtfulness, or because they are in their dotage, but rather because we make it hard for such people to be heard. This book is a contribution to that task.

Appendix
The Elderly in Britain: Statistics

The recent upsurge of interest in the elderly, notably in the provision of services for the elderly and for the frail elderly in particular, has been sparked by a recognition of the growth in their numbers. In Britain today there are over ten million people of pensionable age (that is, women of 60 and over, and men of 65 and over). Although more male babies are born than female, and young men outnumber young women, more men than women die each year so by the age of 50 there is equilibrium between the sexes. From that age onwards there are more women than men, and within the population of people over 65, women outnumber men by five to three. These differences in the sex ratio are even more marked in the older population, where women make up more than two-thirds of people aged 75 years and over. This can be seen from the age–sex pyramid of the British population in 1984 on the following page.

Not only has the absolute number of elderly people increased, but the proportion of elderly people within the total population has also increased. This ageing of the population is a comparatively recent trend in industrialised societies and is the result not only of a decrease in the mortality rate of all ages, but also because the general decrease in the birth rate means that there are proportionally fewer children and proportionally more elderly within the population. During this century the numbers of people over 65 has increased from 1.7 million to 8.4 million, and the proportion of the population aged 65 and over has increased from 5 per cent to 15 per cent. This

Population by sex and age, 1984

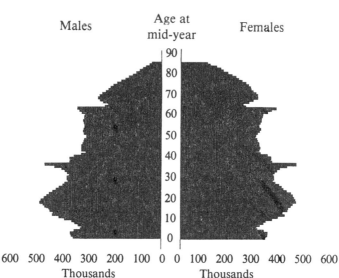

Source: Office of Population Censuses and Surveys; Government Actuary's Department.

increase in both absolute and proportional numbers of elderly people is expected to continue into the next century.

Furthermore, within this age group there is likely to be an ageing of the elderly population itself. During the 1980s and

% Population 65 +

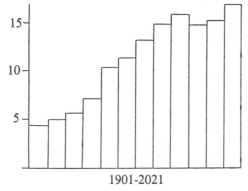

1901-2021

Source: Family Policy Studies Centre: An Ageing Population

1990s the numbers in the younger retirement age group will decline due to the fall in the number of births in the 1920s and 1930s. So although the projected percentage increase between 1981 and 2001 is 4 per cent for all persons over 65, the numbers of people aged 75 years and over are expected to increase by 28 per cent. Increases among the very elderly are even more marked: in these 20 years the numbers of those over 85 are expected to double from half a million to one million people.

Population Projections

	1971	1981	1991	2001	2011	2021
WOMEN						
60—64	1.5	1.4	1.3	1.3	1.6	1.6
65—74	2.4	2.6	2.5	2.3	2.4	2.8
75—84	1.3	1.6	1.7	1.7	1.6	1.8
85+	0.3	0.4	0.6	0.7	0.8	0.8
MEN						
65—74	1.8	2.0	2.0	1.9	2.0	2.3
75—84	0.6	0.8	1.0	1.1	1.0	1.2
85+	0.1	0.1	0.2	0.3	0.3	0.4

Source: Mid 1981 Pop. projections: OPCS monitor PP2 83/1

Many more people can now expect to live to see their grand-children grow to adults, and witness the birth of their great-grandchildren. Also, many more people will reach retirement with their own parents still alive. Increasingly, we can expect the 'young old' to be looking after the very old.

Marital status

Women tend to live longer than men and to marry men a few years older than themselves, so that a much larger proportion of older women are widows compared to the proportion of men who are widowers. The prevalence of widows is increased among the present generation of pensioners by the effects of the deaths of so many young men during both world wars, thereby decreasing the number of older women who are likely to be married. Figures for 1984 show that 36 per cent of women over 65 were married, compared to 71.8 per cent of men in this age group. The number of women who are married drops dramatically for those aged 85 and over; in this group, only 7.2 per cent of women were married, although well over one third – 38.6 per cent – of men were married, according to the 1981 census.

Housing

One of the results of the high proportion of older women who are widows is that many live alone. Indeed almost half of all women over 65 live alone; for women aged 85 and over, 53 per cent are living alone. Only 5 per cent live in institutions, the rest live in individual homes. Where and in what type of housing are the elderly living? The push towards owner-occupation of houses has affected the elderly less than other groups. Just under half the people over 65 live in rented accommodation. However, a much higher proportion of those aged 75 and over, who are living alone, live in rented accommodation and in particular in privately rented unfurnished accommodation.

> Households which include elderly persons are more likely than those with no elderly members to lack some basic amenity. Elderly persons living alone are most at risk of poor housing condition.[13]

'Retirement'

A further recent change in the circumstances of the elderly which reflects the present economic climate is that of occupational status. In 1982 only 4 per cent of women and 7 per cent

164

of men over 65 were in either full- or part-time employment. This contrasts sharply with the position some 20 years before: in 1959, 6 per cent of women and 29 per cent of men over 65 were in work. This decrease in the numbers working past retirement age is a reflection of the growth in the overall level of unemployment, coupled with incentives for early retirement. This period has also shown a growth in the numbers of women of pensionable age who are 'retired workers', from 9 per cent to 25 per cent, reflecting the growth in female employment in the 1960s and 1970s.[14] Both these trends will have a great impact on the life-style of many older people, with more men and women making the decisive break with the world of work on reaching pensionable age. Past employment status also has an impact on the current income of many pensioners.

Income

It is extremely difficult to produce accurate statistics on the income of retired people as the information derives from a variety of sources. For instance, we know how many pensioners receive state pensions and supplementary benefit, but we do not know for how many this is a sole source of income. Some pensioners will receive a graduated pension, although this scheme was abandoned in 1973. Occupational pensions are an increasing source of income, at least for male pensioners, but while we know the numbers of working people paying into occupational pension schemes it is difficult to ascertain how many of today's pensioners benefit from such a scheme, or the level of any such income. An estimation of the main sources of pensioners' income is included in an article by G.C. Fiegehen for the Economic Advisor's Office in the D H S S[15]: and is reproduced below.

At present, 9.3 million people are in receipt of state retirement pensions; 6.1 million women and 3.2 million men. However, because of the low level of this state pension, many people, for whom this is the sole source of income, are also

165

Main components of pensioners total income for Great Britain 1984-5

	%
Income from the state (retirement pension and social security benefits)	60%
Occupational pensions	22%
Earnings	9%
Investment	9%

eligible for supplementary benefit. Of course we don't know the numbers who are eligible, but we do know that at present almost 1.8 million pensioners claim supplementary benefit; of these the vast majority (72 per cent) are women (source: Social Security statistics). These, then, are people who are acknowledged to have an income that is not a sufficient one. Not only does this group of people have a low income, they also have almost no wealth. Currently, savings of £3000, which is not an enormous nest-egg to last for perhaps 30 years of retirement, prohibits any claim on supplementary benefit, no matter how low the level of current income.

Notes

1. 'A Finger in the Apple Pie', *Guardian*, 6 March 1985.
2. S. Parker, *Older Workers and Retirement*, H.M.S.O., 1980.
3. M. Szinovacs (ed), *Women's Retirement – Policy Implications of Recent Research*, Sage Publications, 1982.
4. B. MacDonald and C. Rich, *Look Me in the Eye*, The Women's Press, 1984.
5. H. Roberts (ed), *Doing Feminist Research*, Routledge and Kegan Paul, 1981.
6. J. Finch, 'It's Great to Have Someone to Talk to', in C. Bell and H. Roberts (eds), *Social Researching, Politics, Problems, Practice*, Routledge and Kegan Paul, 1984.
7. A. Oakely, 'Interviewing Women: A Contradiction in Terms', in H. Roberts (ed), *Doing Feminist Research*, Routledge and Kegan Paul, 1981.
8. *ibid*.
9. M. Sarton, *As We Are Now*, The Women's Press, 1983.
10. R.M. Butler and M.I. Lewis, *Aging and Mental Health*, Mosby, 1983.
11. J. Bornat, C. Phillipson and S. Ward, *A Manifesto for Old Age*, Pluto Press, 1984.
12. B. MacDonald and C. Rich, *Look Me in the Eye*, The Women's Press, 1984.
13. Family Policy Studies Centre, *An Ageing Population*, Fact Sheet, 1984.
14. M. Abrams, 'Changes in the Lifestyles of the Elderly

1959–82', *Social Trends*, Vol 14, 1984.

15. G.C. Fiegehen, 'Income After Retirement', *Social Trends*, Vol 16, 1986.

Barbara Macdonald & Cynthia Rich
Look Me In The Eye

**'As I enter my 72nd year, the book has come as a
revelation, hitting me with the shock of recognition.'**

Look Me in the Eye is about the aging of women, and the
prejudice that permeates even the language we use to describe
it. The authors accuse us of denying our own fears about age, and
colluding in a social conspiracy to make old women 'invisible'. In
inviting us to look each other in the eye, they ask us to reclaim the
strength, the wisdom and the sorrow of old women for ourselves.

'Extremely rarely does a book actually change lives, open
doors and affect the human condition. I believe that this one
should and will' May Sarton

Social Studies/Women's Studies £2.95
ISBN: 0 7043 3945 5

Rosemary Manning
A Corridor of Mirrors

An Autobiography

Rosemary Manning combined a successful public career as a
school headmistress and author of a variety of novels for adults
(including *The Chinese Garden*, reissued by Brilliance Books in
1984) and story-books for children – the well-loved 'Dragon'
books *Green Smoke*, *Dragon in Danger*, *The Dragon's Quest*
and *Dragon in Harbour* are all still in print with Puffin.

Yet until recently a central fact of Rosemary Manning's life –
her lesbianism – she kept secret, even publishing her bravely
honest autobiographical *A Time and A Time* (written in the
1960s, when she was in her fifties) under a pseudonym. Now
this fine writer has produced a second autobiography, putting
her political and personal experience into a new perspective.
She deals with her early hopes for a changed world through
socialism, her relationships with friends and lovers, and her late
and, as she feels, crucial, encounter with the women's movement.

Autobiography £5.95
ISBN: 0 7043 4054 2

May Sarton
As We Are Now

**'I am not mad, only old, I make this statement to give
me courage. To give you an idea what I mean by
courage, suffice it to say that it has taken two weeks
for me to obtain this notebook and a pen. I am in a
concentration camp for the old, a place where people
dump their parents or relatives exactly as though it
were an ash can.'**

This is the voice of Caro Spencer, seventy-six, a former
teacher of mathematics, a woman who has prided herself in
her independence of spirit and the liveliness of her intellect.

Now, abandoned in a home for old people, she can see only
brutality and humiliation around her. She struggles to salvage
what dignity she can through defiance and contempt. But in
the end it is her own inner life that must save her, and the
spark of human love.

In *As We Are Now* May Sarton has written a classic work of
imagination about the nightmare of old age – and the courage
of a woman who manages to turn the nightmare into a victory.

Fiction £3.95
ISBN: 0 7043 3921 8